THOMAS FOWELL BUXTON AND THE LIBERATION OF SLAVES

Thomas Fowell Buxton and the Liberation of Slaves

by
Oliver Barclay M.A., Ph.D.

William Sessions Limited
York, England

© Oliver Barclay 2001

ISBN 1 85072 262 5

Printed in 11 on 12 point Plantin Typeface
from Author's disk
by Sessions of York
The Ebor Press
York YO31 9HS, England

Contents

Chapter		Page
	Preface	vi
	Illustrations	ix
	Chronological Table	x
1.	Wilberforce, Clarkson, Buxton and Liberation	1
2.	Home, University and Quaker Influences	18
3.	Marriage, Employment and Christian Faith	28
	Poverty and Education concerns	
	Prisons and Elizabeth Fry	
4.	In Parliament	42
	His Priorities. Work on the Criminal Code and Capital punishment, Prisons and Convict Ships	
	Wilberforce urges him to tackle Liberation	
5.	The Liberation Cause Adopted	53
	Buxton's Team, Clarkson and Macaulay, Sierra Leone	
6.	Parliamentary Battles, Chiefly on Slavery	66
	Slavery, Suttee, Mauritius and South African Blacks	
	Catholic Emancipation	
7.	The Final Battle on Slavery	81
	Division amongst supporters. The Reform Bills. Victory.	
	Apprenticeship of the slaves, Irish Tithes Bill	
8.	A Final Attack on the continuing Slave Trade	108
	The Niger Expedition. Apparent Failure and Buxton's Death. His Character	
9.	Long Term Results of Liberation and the Niger Expedition	131
	Notes	143
	Bibliography	152
	Index	155

Preface

BY ANY STANDARDS the liberation of all the slaves in the British Colonies in 1834 was an extremely important event in British and Colonial history. In many ways it also represented a victory of moral principle over economic power. The processes by which it was achieved and the difficulties that were encountered are full of interest today, especially to anyone trying to support a moral issue that needs legislation.

In recent literature concerned with the anti-slavery campaigns the emphasis has almost always been on the great battle for the abolition of the British Slave Trade and Wilberforce's outstanding leadership in it. The second campaign, for the Liberation of the slaves, only started in Parliament fourteen years after the abolition of the Trade. It was equally fiercely contested, but is not often given equal attention. This book is an attempt to show how important and difficult that second task was and to describe the chief characters in the battle and in particular to provide a biography of the leader of it in Parliament, Thomas Fowell Buxton.

Buxton, who carried the Liberation Act through Parliament in 1833, represents in himself an important tradition of Christian involvement in public life. I hope that this study may give some encouragement to those who, similarly, want to give their energies to meeting the needs of the disadvantaged, but find that it is not as easy as it sounds and look for examples of how others have succeeded. Buxton wrote: 'My mission is evidently not abroad, but is no less a mission on that account'. He saw a political role as essentially a sphere of public usefulness and did not care greatly about his reputation. His family motto was 'Do it with your might' and he needed, and possessed, unusual perseverance in the tasks that he set himself and ability to cope with the criticisms that he met from all sides. Many of the problems that confronted him, as well as his older friend William Wilberforce before him, are almost duplicated today. It emerges that in principle his political world was not so different from ours as one might expect. If these men had wanted one biblical verse to describe their motivation it could have been the Apostle Paul's exhortation: 'As we have opportunity, let us do good to all people'. They did have opportunity and regarded that as giving them a responsibility to act.

There has been no substantial biography of Buxton for a long time, partly because his voluminous papers were not available in public until 1975. It therefore seems worthwhile to re-tell the story, particularly as it relates to the liberation of the slaves, and to include some comments on the longer term results of that and the other programmes that he promoted.

I have to acknowledge my debt to many people. My wife was the first to suggest that the story be re-written, when she read the 'Memoirs of Sir Thomas Fowell Buxton', edited by his son Charles. Professor Howard Temperley provided the next stimulus by sending me a copy of his study of the Niger Expedition, when he was told of my interest in Buxton. I am very grateful for that. I need also to acknowledge my thanks to various descendants of T.F.Buxton for lending me copies of long out of print memoranda of his wife and daughters and other relatives, which were mostly published for private circulation. Mrs Verily Anderson Paget, whose studies are based on family records that are not all publicly available, supplied some material. Mrs E.R.C. Creighton, also a descendant, lent me a batch of MS letters to and from Buxton which are only now about to be made publicly available. The very big collection of Buxton's papers, which were well organised by his daughter, are now available, to those who can get there, in the Rhodes House Library at Oxford. I am grateful to them for giving me access. These I have consulted, though they, and apparently a very large number of other papers, were available to his son Charles when he wrote his 'Memoirs' of his father. Some of the best material at Rhodes House is reprinted in the 'Memoirs'. That book has been a main source of my material. As it ran through a fair number of editions and is not impossible to obtain second hand, I have frequently referred to that rather than to the originals at Rhodes House. Dr John Wolffe gave me important comments on an early draft of most of it and Professor Temperley advised me on the last chapter when that was in an early draft. Professor Andrew Walls has allowed me to use materials from his as yet unpublished 1997 Easneye Lectures on 'The Legacy of Thomas Fowell Buxton', as well as offering me materials in conversation and in some of his papers. I also want to thank the staff at Sessions of York, especially Mr Bob Sissons, for their helpfulness and speedy action.

Finally I must thank my wife, Daisy, for her continual help and comments as she read more than one draft for me, encouraged me to keep at the work and tolerated my preoccupation with it when she had a right to expect me to be more free for other things.

Illustrations

I ACKNOWLEDGE WITH thanks the courtesy of the permissions given below to reproduce the illustrations:
Cover illustrations: Portrait of T.F. Buxton: Lord Buxton. Kneeling slave medallion by courtesy of the Trustees of the Wedgwood Museum, Barleston, Staffordshire.

	Page
Portrait of William Wilberforce. THE WITT LIBRARY, COURTAULD INSTITUTE OF ART	7
Portrait of Thomas Clarkson. THE WISBECH AND FENLAND MUSEUM, WISBECH	7
Plan of the Slave ship *The Brookes*. ANTI-SLAVERY INTERNATIONAL	15
Portraits of Thomas Fowell Buxton, Hannah Buxton and Elizabeth Fry. LORD BUXTON	29
The Brewery of Hanbury and Buxton in Brick Lane. MRS VERILY ANDERSON PAGET	36
A convoy of slaves. MARY EVANS PICTURE LIBRARY, LONDON	64
Northrepps Hall. MRS E.R.C. CREIGHTON	79
The House of Commons, 5th February 1833. NATIONAL PORTRAIT GALLERY, LONDON	94
Anti-Slavery Meeting in Exeter Hall. MARY EVANS PICTURE LIBRARY, LONDON	113
The ship Wilberforce. NATIONAL MARITIME MUSEUM, GREENWICH, LONDON	122

Chronological Table

1772	Granville Sharp obtains judgement that all slaves living in UK are legally free.
1780	Wilberforce enters Parliament aged 21.
1783	Quaker Committee set up to raise concern about slavery.
1786	Wilberforce, after conversion, persuaded to stay in Parliament.
	Clarkson devotes his life to the cause of the slaves.
1787	Sierra Leone set up as a 'Province of Freedom'.
1789	Wilberforce persuaded to take up the cause of the slaves in Parliament and obtains a Privy Council Committee on the Trade. Liberation left on one side.
1791	Wilberforce's first motion on *Abolition of the Trade*. Defeated.
1792	519 Petitions sent to Parliament. Wilberforce's second motion defeated.
1793	French King killed and all reform under suspicion. Further motions delayed after another defeat.
1796	Wilberforce's new motion lost by 4 votes and several other motions lost in later years.
1807	*Final Victory on the Trade. The British Trade to stop in 1808.*
1807-1820	Efforts to stop other countries carrying on the Trade. No activity in Parliament on Liberation.
1818	Buxton becomes an MP aged 32 and is soon prominent in reform of the penal code.
1822	Buxton, persuaded by Wilberforce, agrees to lead the campaign for *Liberation of the Slaves*.
1823	Buxton's first motion on liberation, diluted by the government and then defeated.

1823-4	Start of new public campaign led by friends outside Parliament, especially Clarkson. Government urges Colonies to mitigate slavery and they do nothing. Partial measures create unrest in Colonies and consequent adverse reaction at home.
1824-28	Government repeatedly advises Colonies to curb excesses, but without effect. Wilberforce leaves Parliament sick (1925). Motions on liberation defeated. Buxton constantly harrying the Cabinet, who are preoccupied with other issues but gradually realise that they must pacify the public and the Parliamentary group.
1830 and 1832	At elections candidates made to declare their position on slavery and results published to voters in many areas. Very large local meetings and many petitions to Parliament. Big public campaign by slave interests against liberation.
1832	Following the passage of the Reform Bill, bringing many more voters onto the roll, more new MPs elected with sympathy for liberation. Buxton defeated again, but Government admits that it must propose liberation soon.
1833	After further delays Government finally produces a Bill requiring concessions (including apprenticeship) from Buxton and his group in Parliament. Aug. 28th. Act for the *Total Abolition of Colonial Slavery* becomes Law. Wilberforce after illness dies as it is going through Parliament.
1833-4	Buxton and others work to train teachers for Christian education of freed slaves.
1834	Aug. 1st. *All slaves in British Dominions free people!* Totally peaceful celebrations.
1837-40	Niger Expedition planned to start the defeat of remaining Slave Trade by commerce.
1838	Apprenticeship ends. Complete freedom.

1840	Prince Albert supports the Niger Expedition at Exeter Hall public promotion.
1841	January. Niger Expedition sails and by December has failed.
1845	Buxton dies.
1861-65	American Civil War ends slavery there. Much bloodshed and destruction.
1868	Atlantic Slave Trade officially ended by all participant countries.

CHAPTER 1

Wilberforce, Clarkson, Buxton and Liberation

ON AUGUST 7th 1833 the British Parliament passed an Act voting £20,000,000 (an enormous sum in those days) for the liberation of all slaves in the British Colonies. This was the climax of a nation-wide and hard fought battle spread over more than 50 years, first against the Slave Trade and then for the Liberation of the slaves themselves. In Parliament Wilberforce led the way against the Trade, but then became too frail to do much more and passed the leadership against slavery itself to Thomas Fowell Buxton, who headed up the Liberation campaign for the 12 years up to this victory. The case was won against enormous vested interests and in the face of predictions that when freed the slaves would riot in drunkenness, refuse to work and rise up in violence and take vengeance on their previous masters. Not even all Church leaders were agreed that it was the right thing to do; yet a long and carefully planned programme of petitions, public meetings and distribution of literature, supporting a group of MPs harrying an unwilling government, had ensured that in the end the government dared not oppose it and finally made it their own measure.

All slaves were to be liberated a year later at midnight on August 1st 1834. On that day 800,000 slaves ceased to be property, bought and sold at market like cattle, subject to arbitrary and often very cruel punishments and with no standing at law. They became citizens, able to own property, maintain their marriages and families, put their children in school, give evidence in court and plan their own lives. Their children became their own, no longer someone else's property to be sold or abused at pleasure. By any standards it was a colossal achievement. For five anxious weeks there was no news in Britain of what had happened. When at last the first ships arrived with letters and reports from the Colonies the news could hardly have been better. The churches throughout the slave colonies had been packed with expectant slaves and at the sound of midnight their only response had been united praise and thanksgiving to God followed by cheerful celebration. They continued to work and nowhere had there been revenge, neither had the owners misbehaved. The strategy of the 'Liberation Party' had been overwhelmingly successful. A peaceful settlement had been achieved and against the demands of some of the more idealistic anti-slavery advocates, who regarded it as outrageous to give the slave owners any compensation and so to 'pay people for a sin'. It is not unfair to compare it with the terrible civil war that was needed to liberate slaves in the whole of the USA. Conditions there were in important ways different but it took another 30 years, that is a whole generation, for liberation to be accomplished in all of the States there.

The Anti-Slavery Campaign

The anti-slavery campaign has been described as 'the first successful large scale human rights campaign'. As such it was more significant than even its own great achievements, because it set an example of how moral issues can be made to win in politics. It has therefore often been an inspiration, and even a model, to others seeking to pursue Christian or other moral influence in public life.

If the liberation of the slaves is seen as the climax of the whole anti-slavery campaign, it is important to realise that it was only won after a long battle of over more than 60 years, and involving many people outside Parliament as well as those well known ones who were in Parliament. The campaign against the Slave Trade and that for the Liberation of the Slaves, separated by fourteen years, are often confused because the word 'abolition' has been used for both. To avoid this we shall confine the word abolition to the abolition of the Trade and use the term liberation for the freeing of the slaves. In USA, and at the time in Britain, the term emancipation was commonly used for liberation.

The liberation of the slaves was in some ways only the middle point of a campaign that continues almost to today. There were three distinct phases of these battles in Britain, each having a distinct focus on a different target, though the overall aim was the same. The first phase was against the Trade and was led by Wilberforce in Parliament and by Thomas Clarkson outside it. It started in 1772 and only came to success 35 years later in 1807. The second, for liberation, was mounted in 1821. It was led by Buxton in Parliament and again by Clarkson with others in the general public, coming to victory after 12 years in 1833, that is 24 years after the abolition of the Trade. The third was the attempt to undermine the continuing Trade by introducing constructive and wholesome trade so as to make it more worthwhile for the African chiefs to employ *free* labour and get involved in commerce rather than slave trading. Buxton led this effort at first, but his initial attempts in 1840 were an apparent failure and he died in 1845. His ideas were however taken over by others, famously by David Livingstone in East Africa. That task was never totally finished and the Atlantic Trade continued to 1868 and the East African Trade, by Arab traders, into the twentieth century in some areas.

The Battle against the Trade – Wilberforce and Clarkson

All great campaigns are much more than the prominent individuals who lead them and this is patently true of the anti-slavery movement. Many people played important parts in it, passing on their roles to others as time went by. Even after the British Slave Trade had been ended in 1807, there was an enormous amount left to do before it was ended world wide.

A number of philosophers and theologians had expressed their objections to the Slave Trade, and to slavery itself, during the Eighteenth Century, but there seemed little that could be done about it. It had been a main source of labour in many countries for centuries. The prosperity of Bristol, Liverpool and several other very important British and continental cities depended on it and the opponents of abolition frequently warned of national economic disaster and widespread ruin and unemployment if it was stopped. There were very powerful vested interests both inside and outside the British and other continental Parliaments to make it seem an impracticable ideal. No one seemed to give it enough priority to do anything until a group of largely evangelical Christians made anti-slavery their chief concern. Apart from the Quakers no denomination as a whole committed themselves to the campaign, though the General Baptists passed a resolution supporting it a little later. It was a pressure group of mainly laymen, from a variety of Churches, who carried the day.

The first public blow was struck by an Anglican lawyer, Granville Sharp. He seems to have been regarded as slightly eccentric, but you probably needed to be eccentric then to take on a huge public and economic institution single handed. He fought for a legal decision on the legitimacy of slave owning in Britain. In 1772, after several attempts, he obtained a ruling from the Lord Chief Justice, Mansfield, that effectively made slave owning on British home ground illegal. This did not affect the Colonies and did nothing to stop the Slave Trade between Africa and the Americas, even when this was carried on by British ships operating out of British ports. Mansfield was himself a slave owner and tried to avoid an outright declaration that it must cease, but the effect was that several thousand slaves in Britain, many of them domestic servants, were given freedom, and it signalled that British law was likely to be on the side of freedom.

At the same time the Quakers in Britain had been discussing the matter and were stirred into fresh action by American Quaker writers, notably John Woolman and Anthony Benezet, whose works were circulated by them and then reprinted in Britain. These influenced others outside the rather self-enclosed circle of the Quaker communities and, for instance, John Wesley in 1774 wrote a book against slavery that depended heavily on one of Benezet's.[1]

The London Quarterly Meeting of the Quakers decided that no Quaker should own slaves or take part in the Trade and in 1783 set up a permanent Committee to try to find ways of exerting influence in the matter, starting with a petition to Parliament. While Quakers were growing in importance, they probably had no more than 50,000 members at the time and their rule against 'marrying out' prevented their influence spreading widely into other denominations. They had no MPs until 1833. Throughout the campaigns, however, it must be recorded that they played an extremely important and very consistent part in agitations outside Parliament and initiated many petitions to Parliament. In many ways a large number of largely unknown Quakers were the leaders in the whole process. This included their women, who, unusually for that generation, led the way in creating ladies associations, which added greatly to the spread of anti-slavery ideas.

The next step forward came with the appearance on the scene of Thomas Clarkson (1760-1846)[2], an ordained Anglican. After ordination as a Deacon and as a graduate student at Cambridge he had entered for a Latin essay prize and won it. That year (1785) the Vice Chancellor of the University, Dr Peckard, who held anti-slavery views, had set as the topic: 'Is it lawful to make slaves of others against their will'. Clarkson set to work to research the topic about which he says he knew almost nothing. He relied heavily on the same book by Anthony Benezet and was shocked by what he discovered about the Trade. The horrors were little known in public and the traders tried to make it all seem harmless. On a journey from Cambridge to London he stopped on the hill north of Wadesmill to rest his horse and thought about it all. He says that he saw that 'if the contents of the Essay were true, it was time some person should see these calamities to the end'. He went home much distressed by the facts he had collected and after further thought decided that he must make this his crusade and give himself to the cause of the slaves. There is a small monument on the side of the old A10 road to mark the spot. He never proceeded to full ordination training and most of the rest of his life was preoccupied with fighting this gross evil. It became his consuming passion. He translated his Latin essay into English, found a Quaker publisher, James Phillips, to publish it in an expanded edition, and it soon reached a very considerable and influential readership.

When a little later he discovered the Quakers' interest in the subject he was delighted as he, like many others, was quite unaware of their concern. The Quaker Committee was then expanded in 1787 to include Clarkson and some other non-Quakers, with Granville Sharp as Chairman. This committee soon had 30 members, including James Phillips and Josiah Wedgwood the Quaker pottery manufacturer. From then on the programme began to develop into a national campaign to arouse public concern, using the network of Quaker communities as a starting point in most areas. Clarkson travelled the country tirelessly to collect more detailed and absolutely reliable facts and to stir people up. Finally he expended most of his money in the effort and ran himself into a sort of breakdown in 1793. He retired to the Lake District for ten years, married and then re-emerged again as a very active worker to revive the campaign. In the Lake District he became a close friend of his neighbour, William Wordsworth, and got to know the poet Coleridge, who was to describe him as 'a giant with one idea' and the 'moral engine of the campaign'.

Very few people apart from the slavers themselves realised just how horrendous the Trade was and traders denied cruelty. The committee, fed with facts by Clarkson, issued thousands of pamphlets, leaflets and a number of books, including a major one by Clarkson himself. Josiah Wedgwood issued a cameo of a kneeling slave in chains and the words 'Am I not a man and a brother'. This became a sort of badge of the campaign, placed prominently in even humble cottages and worn by smart ladies of fashion in gold. Clarkson rejoiced that for once fashion helped the cause! He discovered a plan of a slave ship and published a sheet, showing how the slaves were packed like sardines. This was given enormous publicity and horrified the public. He had to find reliable witnesses, willing to speak in public about the horrors of the Trade, and some of them withdrew their evidence when threatened by traders. He himself seems to have been in serious danger at times. He was a superb organiser, while Wilberforce was not! All this was not without fierce opposition. The pro-Slave Trade advocates also issued a few posters and leaflets, and presented some counter-petitions with numerous violent letters to the press.

All the public enthusiasm that Clarkson and the committee aroused could however do little to change things without a group and powerful leader in Parliament. Clarkson was introduced to the fairly recently converted Wilberforce and was one of the chief people who helped Wilberforce to see the campaign against the Trade as his great responsibility. William Pitt, the Tory Prime Minister, also encouraged him to do so, as he was very sympathetic to the cause, though he seems to have rather weakened his support later. The Cabinet however was so divided on the matter that it could not be made government policy, however much Pitt might have wished it, and he died in January 1806 before the final motions came before Parliament. His successor, Lord Grenville, was more successful in getting the Cabinet to agree and it was finally passed in 1807 as a government measure. The debate closed with universal praise for Wilberforce as the leader of the cause and a standing ovation, which found Wilberforce with head bowed and with tears streaming down his face.

The Wilberforce story is fascinating and has been given several good recent treatments in substantial books.[3] Wilberforce (1759-1833) is rightly well known for his victory on the Slave Trade, but he had a number of other philanthropic and moral programmes. In a day when political parties were much less well defined than today he was an 'independent' MP but had a close friendship with William Pitt and sat with the Tories. He entered Parliament in 1780, aged 21, as the MP for Hull, but in 1785 he experienced an evangelical conversion, through reading the New Testament and Doddridge's *Rise and Progress of Religion in the Soul,* as he toured Europe with an evangelical friend and discussed it with him. At first this led him to think of leaving politics, but he was persuaded by the preacher and Hymn writer, John Newton, whom he consulted, that he should stay in it and use his gifts there to see where he could do good. Newton had himself been a slaver before his conversion and only a little later seems to have encouraged him to

Left: William Wilberforce in 1808, soon after the passing of the abolition of the Slave Trade.
Right: Thomas Clarkson in his prime, probably about 1800.

take on the anti-slave trade cause. Wilberforce was socially charming and was described by Mme de Stael as 'the wittiest converser in England'. He was also a brilliant parliamentary speaker, called 'the nightingale of the House of Commons' and had held their attention for speeches of more than three hours. For most of his career he was the MP for the very influential constituency of Yorkshire. He had a remarkable group of fellow workers who are today often referred to as 'The Clapham Sect' or 'the men of Clapham' because they either lived in Clapham or were constant visitors there. The wealthy banker, Henry Thornton, was generally the host for their frequent meetings to plan various philanthropic activities and Wilberforce moved to live next door to him. He was Wilberforce's cousin.

Wilberforce, with the support of Pitt, first managed to obtain a Privy Council 'Committee of Enquiry' into the Trade, though its conclusions were confused. His first motion for abolition was proposed in 1789 and, like his numerous further motions, was defeated. He regularly put forward proposals, year after year, only leaving the matter to one side for a few years when, after the execution of the French King and 'the terror' in Paris, all ideas of 'liberty' came under suspicion. The final victory in 1807 was rightly greeted as a personal triumph and his reputation rose to give him a position of great influence on moral issues in the nation. He was described as 'the nation's conscience' and was able to further several other moral and philanthropic causes. He inevitably attracted a good deal of caustic criticism, being called a hypocrite and other names in the press and charged, quite unjustly, with not caring for the poor at home.

Wilberforce then discovered that, as his opponents had predicted, other countries took over much of the Trade and it continued little diminished. In fact it is estimated that it increased slightly for the first few years (see Chapter 9). As Britain had been the largest player in the Trade it was assumed that there would be a massive decline. He and his fellow workers became preoccupied with trying to get other nations to follow the British example, getting the government to offer them large sums of money to do so, and trying to get abolition written into the Treaties after the Napoleonic wars. This preoccupied him and Clarkson went to Paris to try to persuade the leaders of other nations to write abolition into the Treaties. Clarkson was given interviews with the Russian Emperor and other national leaders. William Allen, an internationally respected intellectual Quaker, was sent next for similar personal interviews, but neither of them had any success The abolitionists were also encouraging the British government to maintain and if possible strengthen the very expensive Naval task force on the West Coast of Africa, which was trying to police the ban against rogue British traders and ships of other nations.

Wilberforce wanted liberation earnestly. In 1818 he wrote to J.J. Gurney: 'Emancipation ...has ever been and still is both the real and the declared Object of all the friends of the African Race'[4]. Nevertheless, in order to get the Trade ended, he had had to say repeatedly in Parliamentary debates that he was not proposing it, on one occasion carelessly seeming to imply that he did not have it in his aims. In fact as the Abolition Act was going through Parliament in 1807 he had actually opposed a sudden additional motion from a young and inexperienced MP that liberation should be added to it. Wilberforce realised that this could have resulted in the House of Lords vetoing the whole Act. As a result he could hardly turn round immediately to propose liberation. In any case there was a lot still to do to get other countries to follow the British lead and abolish their Trade and, when later he did speak for it, he was charged with hypocrisy or duplicity. This also may have restrained him a little. Some of these attacks were quite ferocious. *The Times* for instance published a letter that said:

> Wilberforce skulking from his *original and solemnly recorded pledge*, never to propose the abolition of slavery, sheltered himself under the shadow of the philanthropist brewer Fowell Buxton.[5]

Wilberforce had not in fact promised that he would never propose liberation, only that he was not proposing it at that time. Like the rest of the anti-slavery activists he saw the whole process as one. He was repeatedly open that he would love to see liberation, but it had been widely believed that the abolition of the Trade would inevitably lead to the freeing of the slaves and that in any case the slaves needed some time to be prepared for freedom. There were several reasons why, as he himself acknow-ledged (see Chapter 5), he did not do much for liberation until 1821 and it was 1822, fifteen years after the abolition of the Trade, before a real campaign was begun for liberation with a *Society for the Mitigating and Gradually Abolishing the State of Slavery throughout the British*

Dominions. The word gradually should be noted. It was hoped that education and Christian instruction could lift the slaves from their deprived state, so that they would be better able to cope with freedom, and meanwhile to get the planters to improve their working conditions to allow this. By then, however, Wilberforce was unwell. He had for a long time been successfully dosed with opium by the doctors for his stomach, but as he got older the accumulated effect of the drug began to tell on his health and he had to pass on the leadership of the campaign in Parliament to Buxton. The new and younger group, led by Buxton, were the parliamentary heirs of Wilberforce and his allies. Wilberforce however had to leave Parliament early in 1825 when the battle for liberation there had hardly got going. He continued to speak occasionally at public meetings and helped Buxton and others as much as he could, especially giving advice on the best way to operate in the changing political scene. He died in 1833 as the Liberation Act was going through Parliament.

The Second Phase: Buxton and Liberation

Wilberforce has a number of good recent biographies and the other most important leader, Thomas Clarkson, has two good recent biographical studies, but since Buxton has had no adequate biography for a very long time, we shall give him extended attention and make this study of the liberation campaign also a biography of Buxton. The two are in any case intimately related. Since the liberation campaign and Buxton's part in it have been neglected in the literature, the aim of this study is to remedy that to some extent.

Buxton was also the pioneer in the third phase, and we shall give attention to that in Chapter 8.

It is not always realised that the liberation campaign was at least as difficult as that against the Trade and aroused equally hostile opposition. In fact liberation was in some ways a more difficult target than the Trade. It involved, as the Trade had not, direct interference with the Colonial Legislatures and was seen as an attack on private property. Buxton had little hope of succeeding unless he could persuade the government to make it their own proposal, especially in the House of Lords, where private property was very important. The difference is seen for instance in the fact that the Bishops in the House of Lords voted almost unanimously for the abolition of the Trade but were by no means unanimous on the question of liberation, apparently because they saw it as the first of a series of probable attacks on property, which could fatally undermine the financial position of the Church of England. As a result, while the abolition of the Trade is generally spoken of as a personal achievement of Wilberforce, the liberation of the slaves is sometimes described as one of the achievements of the 'reformed' government under Lord Grey. In fact it was the result of a long fought battle by Buxton and his allies against a very unwilling government, who had frequently frustrated or delayed any action. It had to be a government motion to get it through the Lords. Without that campaign in Parliament, as we shall show, liberation would almost certainly have been very long delayed and might well have been settled only with much bloodshed (as for example in Haiti and USA), and on far less helpful terms for the slaves. The government only gave way in the end for fear of a humiliating defeat on a clearly moral issue. Buxton's part was essential, as Wilberforce's had been on the Trade. Buxton, with public pressure building up outside Parliament, had to create a sufficiently strong liberation party in both Houses of Parliament and then allow the Government to try to gain some credit for such an ethically praiseworthy proposal! No one, unless he has the particular advantages that Wilberforce possessed, could then or now become a real force in the House of Commons in a hurry. Buxton had to learn how the House worked and to earn respect there, by positive successes in other matters, before he could contemplate leading in such a big project.

Neither Wilberforce nor Buxton had a large group of evangelical MPs behind them. In Wilberforce's case it was probably no more than fifteen or twenty. Buxton at one point said that he had only six or so MPs who were 'heart and soul' behind him. Both of them gladly accepted the support of all sorts of people in Parliament, who might differ from them on other matters. Wilberforce, for instance, had the support of the Leader of the Opposition, Charles James Fox, until he died in 1806, although he was publicly known to be someone of dissolute personal morality. The Irish Nationalists also supported Buxton, though many of them were radicals in politics and had spoken up for the French Revolution. What the evangelical nucleus provided was the initiative and then the perseverance to carry it through in spite of competing claims on their time and efforts. While others talked and sometimes sympathised, the leaders kept at it in the face of repeated defeats and frustrations until the job was done, and this largely because they saw it as their God-given task. Buxton, in explaining his reasons for going into politics, said: 'there are plenty of people with more talents, but a great lack of those who love a good cause for its own sake'. This was sadly illustrated in 1796, when a motion proposed by Wilberforce for the abolition of the Trade was defeated by 4 votes, because more than that number of supporters were absent from the debate to attend a new play! Not many were willing to risk much for the cause if the going was tough.

The Wider Influence of the Campaigns and Some Policies Involved

Wilberforce's victory over the British Trade was a huge encouragement to others. It helped greatly towards the worldwide abolition of the Trade and was the first massive victory on the way to the complete defeat of slavery. Buxton could build on what Wilberforce had achieved and could not have succeeded without it, but his own victory was of more immediate benefit to the slaves themselves than the abolition of the British Trade. It also started the process of liberation world wide and added to the confidence of those in other countries, and at home, that moral issues could be made to prevail against vested interests. As the story will show there are reasons why, while Wilberforce is still rightly famous, Buxton is often forgotten.

Wilberforce's victory in Parliament had powerful wider and long term influence. It represented something fairly new in that it demonstrated that moral principles could be made so influential in public life that they overruled money and trade interests in Britain. It gave the confidence needed to persevere in other campaigns. The historian G. M. Trevelyan comments:

> Wilberforce and the anti-slavery men had introduced into English public life and politics new methods of agitating and educating public opinion. The dissemination of facts and arguments: the answers to mis-statements of adversaries on the pleasures of the middle-passage and the happiness of Negro life in the plantations; the tracts; the subscriptions; public meeting – all these methods of propaganda were

systematised by methods familiar enough today but strange and new in that age. The methods of Wilberforce were afterwards imitated by the myriad leagues and societies political, religious, philanthropic and cultural – which have ever since been the arteries of English life.[6]

The leaders of both campaigns had faced many of the same problems as a Christian faces today in politics: When does a political compromise become a moral compromise? How far do your ideals need to be tempered by realism? Can the reformer fight for all the things he values at once, or must he concentrate on one at a time, even though the press will blame him for not attending to their priorities? How should you respond when former supporters denounce you as a compromiser or accuse you of having sold your principles for personal gain? What place should personal ambition have for the Christian in politics? When must you vote against your own party? How far should you try to justify a moral issue in terms of its practical value? Do you actively recruit to your cause people with whom you disagree radically on other issues? The story is full of parallels with present day problems in politics and all of these questions arise as we go through the life of Thomas Fowell Buxton and the campaign for the liberation of the slaves.

Other Nineteenth Century social reformers such as Lord Shaftesbury (earlier as an MP he was Lord Ashley) faced very similar difficulties. When for instance in 1850 Shaftesbury agreed to the government's dilution of the (1847) Ten Hours Bill, to make ten and a half hours a day the limit for the working day, he was furiously denounced by his erstwhile supporters. To them a ten hours principle was sacrosanct. He gave way to the government because he believed that if he did not the whole Bill would be lost, and that once it was on the statute book he could then work to reduce the hours.[7] Nevertheless his reputation with many of his supporters outside Parliament suffered irreparable damage. Fortunately, like Wilberforce and Buxton, reputation was not his great concern.

It is interesting to see some very similar issues arising today in South Africa, Northern Ireland and Israel, where those who want at all costs to keep to their 'principles' or ideals denounce the politicians for trying to get something rather than nothing, and see them as failing to proclaim their ideals in an uncompromising way. Idealists on both sides risk all advance for the sake of maintaining an ideal and so in fact risk bloodshed or long term bitterness and strife. In lesser matters also it is easy to accuse opponents of having lost sight of principles, if they offer to accept some but not all of their aims, as progress towards the ideal. Politics, as has often been said, is the art of the possible. The politician has constantly to balance strong ideals with an understanding of what realistically can be achieved in the circumstances. The reward is to get real advance, even if it is not all that one would have liked. There are not many circumstances in which the ideal can be fully realised.

In some important respects Buxton and Wilberforce, with their associates, were model Christian politicians. They, and the massive public agitations that supported them, helped to put moral issues in the forefront of political debate at a time, not unlike today, when it was generally held that economic forces should determine political ends. Even the High Church leader Pusey regretted the expenditure of £20,000,000 for what he called 'an opinion' or sentiment.[8]

The International Background

It is worth remembering the general historical background to both of the main anti-slavery campaigns. These were far from being years of unruffled peace and prosperity either at home or abroad. The storming of the Bastille, which launched the French Revolution, was in 1789 shortly after Wilberforce's first motion in Parliament was defeated. Those events and the rise of Napoleon and war with France dominated the political scene for nearly 20 years. For two years there had been a serious threat of an invasion of England by the army of over 200,000 collected on the French coast. That threat ended with Trafalgar in 1805. Waterloo in 1815, when Buxton was 29, brought an end to Napoleon's ambitions and gave England a period of military peace in Europe, but ushered in times of unrest at home, with rising poverty and the debates over the Corn Laws.

The French Revolution had profound effects in Britain. On the one hand it led some people into a strongly conservative reaction and a desire to suppress even hints at reform. On the other hand the ideas of 'liberty, equality and fraternity' inspired others towards radical reform. The advocates of the oppressed poor and the Irish Catholics found fresh inspiration and sometimes unwisely associated themselves with the French Revolution, which gave fresh

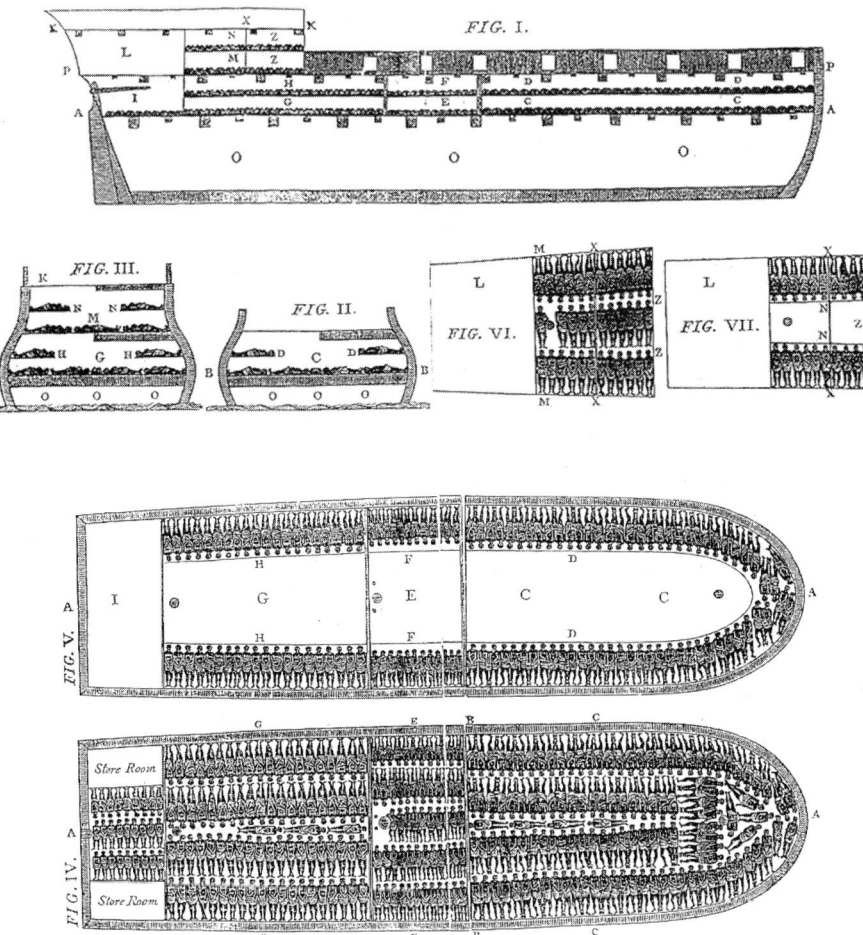

Plan of the Slave Ship The Brookes. *Clarkson published this as a broadsheet and it caused a sensation, as few people had any idea of the conditions on board. It had a huge circulation in various forms. The ship was registered to carry 482 slaves, but had carried 609 on one voyage. Many died on the journey or arrived too sick to live long after it.*

ammunition to their opponents, so that any proposals for reform were liable to be labelled 'Jackobin'. These were turbulent times.

Helpfully the strong input of Non-Conformist influence in many English reform movements reduced the tendency to drift into violence[9]. By the 1820s there was a widespread evangelical influence in many denominations. The Methodists, who had grown greatly in number and influence by 1820, and the other Free Churches, were predominantly evangelical and were of increasing importance in public life, though few of them had the vote. The evangelical parties in the Church of England and the Church of Scotland were also growing. Moral concerns were widespread. Both anti-slavery campaigns depended on such popular morality and anti-slavery provided a focus for much of this concern. There were also many who did not profess to be very religious who shared much of this broadly Christian outlook. Evangelicals provided the primary engine of the prolonged campaigns but their success depended on the moral consensus in the populace at large and in Parliament.

Who then was Buxton and how did he come to carry this responsibility and have the perseverance to carry on a sometimes bitter battle for so long before it came to success? He was a business man and not a career politician like Wilberforce. In fact he had to be persuaded by others that he should enter Parliament in order to use his emerging abilities to tackle some social evils. He took time to learn how to exert any influence in Parliament and to gain enough stature in the eyes of others to be effective. Unlike Wilberforce he did not have the support of any of the Prime Ministers of his time. He had had useful parliamentary experience before he agreed to take on the liberation campaign as his main duty and had a number of other important successes on domestic issues before he came to this his greatest task. Although he was personally popular with people of all levels in society, he did not have the charm and social winsomeness of Wilberforce. He was however a very determined man, with the strength of character needed to do battle for a long time. Buxton never had the enormous influence on public opinion and morality that the older man had. He was more solidly workmanlike in his speeches and probably that was necessary in his generation for the sort of battles he had to wage. Certainly Buxton is not so famous today, but the fact that a statue was erected in Westminster Abbey almost next to that of Wilberforce shows how he was regarded at the time.

The associated names of Wilberforce and Buxton were revered in ex-slave communities in the British Colonies, and huge numbers of very small subscriptions in pennies and halfpennies were given by ex-slaves from the West Indies towards the cost of the Buxton statue. He was a very significant Christian politician and faced many very modern problems. He made mistakes and usually had the grace to acknowledge the fact, but he also had a huge influence for good on vast numbers of people in many countries through his political victories.

CHAPTER 2

Home, University and Quaker Influences

THOMAS FOWELL BUXTON came from that solid squirearchy that provided much of the backbone of the civil service and the Army etc. in days before examinations were introduced. They were not large landowners but usually owned an estate of several farms with the associated cottages for labourers, some woods and waste land with a substantial house that they either built for themselves or had enlarged from an older Manor House or Farm House. Often they were also involved in commerce or trade of some kind, which could make them quite rich. They employed a considerable number of servants, including estate workers and often more than one gamekeeper to police the estate and to maintain a good supply of birds and other game for sport and food. The woods were usually coppiced, by hand labour of course, to provide timber for fencing and fuel and at least incidentally cover for game. The generous hospitality of the big house required an army of servants, and the continuous work of 'hedging and ditching' and other estate maintenance jobs employed not a few. The relationship to their staff and tenants was paternalistic, but at its best included real care for the welfare of their dependants so that, although the huge differences of economic situation were taken for granted as an accepted part of society, acute distress was usually relieved at least to some extent in a way that did not always happen on the really big estates where the landowner was not in the same way confronted with the problems.

Tom's father, the first in the family to be named Thomas Fowell, was one of these relatively small scale landowners with his house at Earl's Colne in Essex, not far from Colchester. He must have been important locally as he served as High Sheriff of the County. He seems to have been a kindly and generous man, but as he died when Tom was six he had little influence on the training of his children. The family were Anglicans and Tom was evidently baptised as a child, though he never made an issue of that. Tom, as he was called as a child, was born on April 1st 1786, the oldest of three brothers and two sisters. When aged 4½ he was sent to a miserable boarding school in Kingston where he was half starved and frequently ill. When his father died he was transferred to a school in Greenwich, which was much better, but where he was not a particularly good scholar and did not work hard. In the holidays there was fishing, shooting and hunting to enjoy and he became a lifelong enthusiast for field sports, though there is no record of his hunting after his childhood.[1]

In this situation the two chief influences on him were his mother and the gamekeeper. The latter could neither read nor write, but was a fund of wisdom and was evidently entrusted with a fair degree of responsibility for disciplining the boy. It was he who gave Tom a life long love of the country, of nature and of country sports. Long afterwards Tom wrote of him:

> My 'guide, philosopher, and friend,' was Abraham Plaistow, the gamekeeper; a man for whom I have ever felt, and still feel very great affection... his memory was stored with various rustic know-ledge. He had more of natural good sense, and what is called mother-wit, than almost any person I have met since... He was the most undaunted of men; I remember my youthful admiration for his exploits on horseback. For a time he hunted my uncle's hounds, and his fearlessness was proverbial. But what made him particularly valuable were his principles of integrity and honour. He never said or did a thing in the absence of my mother of which she would have disapproved. He always held up the highest standard of integrity and filled our youthful minds with sentiments as pure and as generous as could be found in the writing of Seneca or Cicero... Such was my first instructor, and, I must add, my best; for I think I have profited more by the recollection of his remarks and admonition, than by the more learned and elaborate discourses of my other tutors. He was our play-fellow and tutor: He rode with us, fished with us, shot with us on all occasions.[2]

Tom's mother however, was also a great influence. She was the daughter of Osgood Hanbury, a Quaker brewer, and although on marrying Tom's father, who was an Anglican and attending Anglican services, she should have been 'dis-fellowshipped' by Quaker meetings[3], she continued in very warm relations with the network of related Quaker families, who, partly because of the rule against 'marrying out', were repeatedly intermarried and enjoyed a round of social contacts. Also the network of Quaker businesses supported one another in the confidence that they could be trusted as few other people could. In any case Tom's mother remained a Quaker in ethical principles, with a strict morality and a generous attitude to those in need. From later comments it is clear that she shared an abhorrence of slavery and the Slave Trade that was common amongst Quakers. Quakers were also well known for their more than average concern for those that they saw to be in need and their high practical morality. Many Quakers had risen in social status from humble beginnings just because they were trusted by others for their reliability, honesty and concern to sell only things of worthy quality. Members of the Society who fell below these standards were likely to be taken to task by fellow Quakers and even dis-fellowshipped if they did not improve, while if in financial difficulties they also often received advice from experienced members and if necessary financial help if they were capable of recovery.[4] He wrote later:

> My mother was a woman of a very vigorous mind, and possessing many of the generous virtues in a very high degree. She was large-minded about everything; disinterested almost to an excess; careless of difficulty, labour, danger, or expense, in the prosecution of any great object. With these nobler qualities were united some of the imperfections, which belong to that species of ardent and resolute character. My mother... perpetually inculcated on my brothers and sisters that they were to obey me, and I was rather encouraged to play the little tyrant. She treated me as an equal, conversed with me, and led me to form and express my opinions without reserve. This system had its obvious disadvantages, but it was followed with some few incidental benefits. Throughout my life I have acted and thought for myself; and for this kind of habitual decision I am indebted for all the success I have met with.[5]

After eight years at the school in Greenwich he returned home for a year, not much the wiser for his schooling. He spent most of that year aged 14-15 at home in Earls Colne where his mother continued to live until a little later she remarried and moved to near Weymouth as Mrs Edmund Henning. He spent most of that year in sport, a little reading of mostly light literature and generally relaxing. To outward appearances he was on his way to becoming another of the numerous rather well to do pleasure seekers who were looking for a place to be obtained in some adequately paid job through family influence. His mother however wanted him to go to university and at first proposed St Andrews. As a Quaker she did not favour the two English universities in view of their reputation for gambling and dissipation and the requirement that students agree the 39 Articles of the Church of England. These include in Article 37 'It is lawful for Christian men, at the commandment of the Magistrate, to bear weapons, and serve in wars.' Almost all Quakers were by then pacifists and she had some Quaker instincts.

Earlham

At the age of 15 he came into a big change of interests. His mother's sister was married to a well to do Quaker, Richard Gurney of Keswick Hall near Norwich, and he came to know John Gurney (Jnr), one of their nephews from the nearby Earlham Hall, and was invited over to Earlham during this relatively idle year. His mother had evidently visited Keswick Hall often and Earlham sometimes and Tom must have gone with her at least occasionally to Earlham. The impact on Tom of this very relaxed and not very strict Quaker family at Earlham was enormous. There were eleven surviving children (one had died young) and of the seven girls only one was married.[6]

The head of the Earlham family was John Gurney (Snr). He had a significant friendship with Charles Simeon of Cambridge, the leader of a renewed evangelical party in the Church of England. Gurney's wife had died when the oldest child, Catherine, was 17 and she had taken over the running of the household, so much so that she was soon referred to as Mrs Catherine. When finally she handed over the house to her younger brother it was said of her that 'she had governed for 25 years rather as one occupying the presidential chair of a republic.[7] The Earlham family all took Tom under their wing, especially Catherine (now aged 25) and John (Jnr) who was 4½ years older than Tom but was to become a firm friend until he died thirteen years later aged only 33. Tom's attention was however soon caught by the girls! They were an extremely lively and attractive family, living a wide ranging social life, entertaining a variety of interesting people, with a round of dances and enormous dinner parties. The six daughters sang, drew, painted and read aloud to each other from their diaries and a variety of books in the evenings. Catherine made them all write diaries and supervised their education, the older girls teaching the younger children writing, spelling and geography, until in the accepted tradition the boys went to boarding school at age 8 or younger, and the girls continued their education at home, where Catherine got them together on many evenings and read to them from educational and often quite learned books. Augustus Hare in his detailed study of the family depicts a most fascinating and lively family life. On one occasion the girls had linked arms across the main road to hold up the Mail Coach. Visitors ranged from the local landed families and quite poor people, to Prince William of Gloucester[8], and Charles Simeon.

The father, who was in the family wool-stapling business in Norwich, was evidently wealthy, and like a number of other such Quaker families moving increasingly into banking as their reputation for integrity and their resources grew. Although not a strict Quaker, he was committed to the Meeting at Goat's Lane in Norwich and the children all went with him to Sunday meetings there, sometimes with complaints that it was dull and uninspiring. The comment in the diaries: 'Goats was dis', was not infrequent, meaning that it was disgusting. They followed obediently, but were privately unconvinced and far from strict, in a day when being strict meant amongst other things the wearing of very dull coloured clothes (though they could be made attractive), the use of 'thee and thou' in conversation, a studious avoidance of any acknowledgement of titles or deference to status and by men the wearing of a hat, even in the presence of Royalty. Joseph John Gurney, one of the younger brothers, records how when he became a strict Quaker, on one occasion he felt compelled as a matter of conscience to wear his hat as he was greeted by his host. He remarks that he was never invited to dinner parties again.[9] There is a nice description of a reception given by the Queen, surrounded by ladies in elaborate dress and jewellery, at which Elizabeth Fry, neatly dressed in traditional Quaker attire, was the only person who did not curtsy to the Queen. This seems to have resulted in the Queen talking longer to her than to any of the smartly dressed dignitaries present![10] Although these things sometimes gave offence at first, people generally came to accept the idiosyncrasies, but for those who from a less strict background adopted the strict tradition it could be a testing change as Joseph John and some of the other Earlham children found. The father, however, was not so strict that he objected to two of his daughters marrying Anglicans He drew a line when one of them looked likely to marry a Unitarian and told the young man that he was no longer welcome for a year, after which the matter could be reconsidered because the girl was deeply attracted. When the year was up the young man was found to be engaged to someone else. Similarly, he dismissed a Roman Catholic friend who was courting the eldest, Catherine.

He did not, however, control their reading and the Unitarian friend introduced them to David Hume, William Godwin and Tom Paine. The result was that the girls went through a period of scepticism about any Christian beliefs. They were one by one brought back to orthodox beliefs, starting surprisingly with the help of the Roman Catholic friend and his books, and then in several cases the influence of Anglicans. Catherine, who had for a time been in total doubt, was helped by some Moravians to understand the atonement and then clearly converted through a sermon by John Newton, the Hymn writer, at his church in London.[11] She and the others had been reading Hooker and Bishop Butler's *Analogy*, the latter being a special help to her and to her brother Joseph John. In the end several of the family became Anglicans, but Elizabeth (Fry), Joseph John and Priscilla all became recognised 'Ministers' amongst the Quakers, an appointment that was still actively practised at the time. Joseph John was to become one of Tom's closest friends and an active supporter of his work for the rest of his life.

When Tom started visiting Earlham the third daughter, Elizabeth, was already married to a Quaker banker in London, Joseph Fry. She was to become the famous prison reformer and had experienced a striking conversion through the influence of a visiting American Quaker preacher, William Savery, in 1798. After the meeting at 'Goat's' where he preached, Elizabeth asked if she could go back with him alone in the carriage. What was said is not known, but she arrived home a different person and gradually adopted strict Quaker style, to the consternation at first of her sisters. For a while she became quite extreme, giving up dancing, painting and music. This conversion experience marked her whole future work and had a considerable effect on the rest of the family. After a while the thirteen year old Richienda wrote in her journal: 'Betsy seems to be changed from a complete sceptic to a person who has entire faith'. The same sister had commented: 'Betsy's character is certainly, in many respects, extremely improved since she adopted these principles. She is industrious, charitable to the poor, kind and attentive to all of us: in fact if it was not for that serious manner which Quakerism throws over a person, Betsy would indeed be a much improved person.'[12] It influenced all the others to a less frivolous attitude to life. There was until the 1870 Education Act no publicly provided free education and Betsy started a local school for poor children, teaching them to read and write and learn the Bible.

At the time of one of Tom's first visits Elizabeth had been married over a year and was bringing her first born child (the first grandchild) to show her off to the Earlham family. The coach arrived at Earlham amidst great excitement and the third daughter of the house, Hannah, stepped out of the coach with the baby in her arms. Tom who had joined the welcome party was immediately smitten by Hannah, who had been in London with Elizabeth. Many years later he told her that although he had hardly if ever seen her before, he had said to himself: 'She shall be my wife'. How serious this was at 15 one does not know and he became greatly attached to the whole family, who encouraged him to be much more serious in his reading and his whole attitude to life. With little to hold him at his own home he spent a great deal of his free time at Earlham, becoming almost a member of the family. Catherine especially wrote letters of motherly advice, as she did to the others when they left home. A month after this event Tom is writing to his mother:

> Your letter was brought while I was deliberating... Mr Gurney is so good tempered, his daughters are so agreeable, and John so thoroughly delightful, and his conversation so instructive, which is no small matter with you I

know....... Whilst I was at Northrepps, [on holiday with relatives] I did little else but read books of entertainment (except now and then a few hours of Latin and Greek) ride and play at chess. But since I have been at Earlham, I have been very industrious.

A little later he remarks that he has stayed two months at Earlham 'and have got thoroughly acquainted with the most agreeable family in the world'.

University

It now seemed that he had a good hope of inheriting a considerable estate in Ireland. His mother therefore decided that it would be better for him to study in Ireland and it was agreed that he should go to do at least a year's study in Donnybrook, near Dublin, to prepare himself for entrance to the University. This was Trinity College, popularly known as TCD, a Protestant foundation going back to Elizabethan times. It had a good reputation for intellectual liveliness and scholarship, though like Oxford and Cambridge it also included a number of idle rich young men, who lived a fairly dissipated life.

He was the most backward of the group of pupils working under their tutor for the examination, but he immediately set to work with a will and at the end of the year he was the best of the group and successfully passed the entrance standards. He then spent four years aged 17-21 at TCD (1803-1807). These were crucial years and he constantly corresponded with the Earlham family, particularly with John Gurney Jnr and latterly with Joseph John, the youngest but one of the eleven Earlham children. Joseph John was to become a significant influence on Tom as well as on his sisters and brothers. He early adopted strict Quaker style and became a very important evangelical writer and preacher in Quakerism.[13] Tom was also becoming increasingly strongly attached to Hannah and was egged on by her sisters, who carefully left them in a room together, without the desired effect. He wrote to his brother:

> My affair with Hannah goes on as prosperously as I could wish. I am sure she will not refuse me when I make her an offer. I had made a most solemn determination to do so before I left Earlham.....I had one such excellent opportunity, which I shall never forgive myself for being foolish

enough not to take, just before I was going to take my leave, on a sudden and I am sure on purpose, Kitty and all the other girls withdrew, and left me and Hannah alone, I do not know what was the matter with me, but I could no more open my mouth than if I had been struck dumb, so there I sat like a fool till the other girls came back. Did you ever hear of anything so foolish.[14]

They eventually became engaged to be married that year, 1805, but marriage was forbidden by Earlham until he graduated.

In 1803, while at Donnybrook, the Kilwarden rebellion took place, led by the ill fated Robert Emmett. Buxton and his fellow pupils, with loaded pistols, prepared for an attack which never took place, thus initiating him into Irish politics, in a way that was to prove useful to him later as it gave him a vivid reminder of the dissatisfaction of the Catholic population.

At TCD he worked very hard and excelled himself in the examinations ending up with numerous prizes and the Gold Medal, but meanwhile he made the best of the other opportunities available. In April 1805 he writes to Earlham that he had been spending the previous fortnight 'chiefly in reading English Poetry' and that he was going to a schoolmaster to learn reading aloud.

> I have long felt my deficiency in that most useful qualification, especially when I was last at Earlham.... my companions have entertained themselves very much at the idea of my going to school to learn to read. But I expect to gain two very considerable advantages by this plan; the first is, that perhaps it may give you pleasure, and secondly, that as I go immediately after dinner, it will furnish an opportunity for avoiding, without openly quarrelling with, a party of collegians, into whose society I have lately got, and whose habits of drinking make me determine to retreat from them.

He was also elected into the prestigious 'Historical Society', which held debates every week during the last term of the year. Here he gained all four of the available medals, two for eloquence and two for history. Both of these aspects of training were to be of great use later. He wrote to Earlham at the end of his second year in the teasing style that he used often with relatives:

The examinations are over, but alas, I cannot describe the disasters that have befallen me. Think how disagreeable a circumstance it must be to me to have all my hopes disappointed, to lose the certificate, to have my gold medal stopped, and what is worse, to know that my Earlham visit, as it was the cause of my idleness, was the cause of my disgrace. Think of all this, and fetch a very, very, deep sigh, – and look very grave, and then think how happy I must be to tell you that my utmost examinatory hopes are realised... and what is better, that I can ascribe my success to *nothing but my Earlham visit!*

It is extremely doubtful if he would have applied himself so well to study and debating if it had not been for the stimulus of Earlham and this he often gladly acknowledged.

In 1806 he went in the summer vacation for a tour of Scotland with the six unmarried Earlham girls and two other fiancees. There was much reading aloud in the evenings, some practical jokes by the men on the girls and good fun all round. The whole party was interestingly in charge of their drawing master, the almost illiterate John Crome, the founder of the Norwich school of painting. Like Abraham Plaistow this family employee was obviously given a status that far exceeded his immediate responsibilities, as was not uncommon in the relatively unsnobbish Quaker families, even though they mixed freely with the aristocratic community. During this tour Tom bought himself a large Bible and resolved to read it daily, which was clearly a sign that Earlham had not only helped him to do well and read widely but had also begun to have a religious influence on him. He was always a moral young man and he now became serious about his faith, though without any real personal experience.

Buxton, as it is now best to call him, was urged to stand as the MP for Dublin university,[15] which was a very considerable honour. He was likely to have been elected, but he refused, probably partly because he needed to earn some money (MPs were unpaid). His expectations of an Irish inheritance were now seen to be futile, in spite of an expensive law suit pursued by his mother, who had also lost a lot of money through unwise investments.

CHAPTER 3

Marriage, Employment and Christian Faith

WHEN FINALLY HE left TCD and married Hannah in 1807 he was aged 21 and his wife aged 24. He had therefore to look for an income. For a while they were hard up and lived in a cottage near his relatives in the Weymouth area. As he wrote: 'I longed for any employment that would produce me £100 a year if I had to work twelve hour a day for it'.

After a year his two Hanbury uncles invited him to join their brewery firm in London on probation for one year. Good Quakers took nothing for granted! Brewing was seen as socially beneficial when very cheap gin dominated the drinking houses. Some advertised 'Drunk for one penny, dead drunk for twopence'. Water also was not safe and the standard drink in many boarding schools was small beer, that is diluted beer, with enough alcohol to disinfect it. At the brewery he worked extremely hard and started to reorganise the business. He wrote to his mother: 'I was up this morning at four, and do not expect to finish my day's work before twelve tonight – my excuse for silence'. He found carelessness in the books and out of date methods and in 1811 he was made a partner and completed the process of bringing the business up to date, against resistance from some of the older staff. The brewery was in Brick Lane, Shoreditch in the already depressed East End of London and he lived next to the Brewery in a substantial house, now with one child. He visited the homes of his workers in the area and was upset by what he found in the way of poverty and squalor. With his brother-in-law, Samuel Hoare, a very well to do London Quaker banker, he took an active interest in the distressed state of the nearby

Thomas Fowell Buxton. Probably aged about 30.

*Left: Hannah Buxton. The wife of Thomas Fowell Buxton.
Right: Elizabeth Fry.
The two most famous of the 'Gurneys of Earlham' sisters.*

Spitalfields weavers, (the descendants of Huguenot refugees). With William Allen, the Quaker pharmacist in East London,[1] he founded a local school as there was no schooling available. They soon added an adult school and he employed a teacher to teach all his staff to read.

Stimulated by the Gurneys he actively supported the recently created Bible Society, which became a life long concern.[2] It was meeting with considerable opposition from some of the Anglican leaders and for the next few years he entered the controversy and spoke for them repeatedly. In fact it became one of his favourite concerns, delighting in its non-denominational position which upset some Anglicans. William Allen also drew him into a small society which was studying the effects of capital punishment. Increasingly he was becoming interested in and actively involved in meeting social needs.

He found time to join 'The Academics' an informal debating society in London, rather like the Historical Society at TCD. It included at least one old College friend, who with several other members were to become MPs. It also included a former fellow pupil from his Greenwich school, who had in those days done many of his Latin exercises for him! This man, Horace Twiss, a future MP wrote 'I heard, on my first or second evening of attendance, a speech of great ability, from a man of great stature: and I should have been assured that it was my old schoolfellow I saw before me, but I could not suppose it possible so dull a boy could have become so clever a man.'[3] Buxton was a very exceptional six foot four in height and well built. School friends had called him 'Elephant Buxton'.

Each autumn he spent several weeks at Earlham shooting and riding and on one of these visits in 1812 his younger brother-in-law Joseph John Gurney insisted that he should leave his sport for a bit to speak for the Bible Society at a public meeting in Norwich. This was his first public address and, to his own surprise, apparently met with great success.

During this time in Brick Lane (1811) he left the Quaker meeting, to which he had been going with Elizabeth Fry's family, and started attending an Anglican Chapel of Ease. This was the nearby Wheeler Street Chapel, where The Rev. Josiah Pratt, the Secretary of the Church Missionary Society[4] was the preacher.

Pratt was a good teacher of evangelical truth and had a great influence on Buxton's rather vague faith and his wife's. His wife seems to have come first to an assured faith and joined the Church of England by baptism in 1812 under this influence.

One result of Pratt's teaching was a growing dissatisfaction with being so absorbed in business. By 1812 he was writing:

> I know that if success shall crown all my projects, I shall gain what will never satisfy me, 'that which is not bread'. I know the poverty of our most darling schemes – the meanness of our most delicious prospects – the transitoriness of our most durable possessions.... (Yet) I am irritable about trifles, eager about pleasures, and anxious about business: various objects of this kind engross my attention at all times: they pursue me even to Meeting and to Church, and seem to grudge the few moments that are devoted to higher considerations, and strive to bring back to the temple of the Lord the sellers, and the buyers, and the money-changers. My reason tells me that these things are utterly indifferent; but my practice says ,that they only are worthy of attention. My practice says, 'Thou art increased with goods, and hast need of nothing;' but my reason teaches me, 'Thou art wretched and miserable and poor, and blind, and naked'.

Early in the following year he suffered a near fatal illness. It was presumably not helped by the standard practice of blood letting as a remedy. This led to what is best described as an evangelical conversion. From his wife's memoirs[5] it is clearer than from his son's that up to this time he was not certain of some basic Christian doctrines. In particular he had doubts about the Deity of Christ. This had resulted in his being uncertain as to whether he was really forgiven, so that he could not contemplate death with confidence. He knew that he was a sinner and if Jesus was little more than an example then he stood condemned. His doubts may well have arisen from the reading of sceptical books with the girls at Earlham.

In a memoir amongst his papers very soon after he wrote:

> I spent nearly an hour in most fervent prayer. I have been for some years, perplexed with doubts....The object of my prayer was that this perplexity might be removed; and the next day, when I set about examining my mind, I found that it was entirely removed, and that it was replaced by a degree

of certain conviction, totally different from anything I had before experienced. It would be difficult to express the satisfaction and joy which I derived from this alteration. 'Now know I that my Redeemer liveth' was the uppermost sentiment in my mind, and in the merits of that Redeemer I felt a confidence that made me look on the prospect of death with perfect indifference. No one action of my life presented itself with any sort of consolation. I knew that by myself I stood justly condemned; but I felt released from the penalties of sin, by the blood of our sacrifice. In Him was all my trust.

My dear wife gave me great pleasure by repeating this text – 'This is a faithful saying and worthy of all acceptation, that Christ Jesus came into the world to save sinners'.

For the rest of his life this assurance of sins forgiven, because Jesus had died on the cross to bear them, was a frequent theme in his notes and a constant comfort in times of discouragement or awareness of failures and sins.

His wife tells us that during the time of his recovery he had told her that he had for some time: 'felt a sort of lurking doubt which had been as a thorn in his side respecting the truth of the Christian doctrine, that he had thought and prayed much about it in his illness, and that it was shown to him to be truth in the clearest manner'.[6]

On Christmas Day that year he wrote:

In casting up the incidental blessings of the year, I found none to compare with my illness; it gave such a life, such a reality and nearness, to my prospects of futurity; it told me, in language so conclusive and intelligible, that here is not my abiding city. It expounded so powerfully the Scriptural doctrine of the Atonement, by showing what the award of my fate must be, if it depended upon my own merits, and what that love is which offers to avert condemnation by the merits of another: in short, my sickness has been a source of happiness to me in every way.

Far from this experience leading him into an other worldly piety, it provided the perspective on life that enabled him to persevere for the rest of his life and against many difficulties in practical service to others. It also kept him from being swallowed up in business.

His Motives and Priorities

In 1815 he wrote to his wife:

> I fancy that I could brew one hour, study mathematics the next, shoot the third, and read poetry the fourth, without allowing any one of these pursuits to interfere with the others. This habit of full engagement of the mind has its advantages in business and other things, but is attended with this serious disadvantage, that it immerses the mind so fully in its immediate object, that there is no room for thoughts of higher importance and more real moment to creep in. I feel this continually ......How very great a portion of one's life there is, in which one might as well be a heathen!

His dilemma has been shared by many busy Christian professionals down the ages who do not believe that they should withdraw and enter some form of paid Christian ministry. He never developed a sophisticated and well thought out view of the Christian attitude to secular vocations and ambitions. He was not a theological thinker of that kind. Also as he soon only had to devote one or two days a week to the business, he did not feel the pressures as some others, whose daily work was not mostly so directly for the relief of suffering as his parliamentary work was. He did, however, set his priorities in his parliamentary career on service to others rather than promotion or reputation as his subsequent practice showed.

A little later he wrote about money:

> July 7th was an extraordinary day. In the morning I ascertained that all hopes we had indulged of large profits in business were false. We were sadly disappointed, for I went to town in the morning some thousands of pounds richer in my own estimation than I returned at night. This was my first trial; next, about nine o'clock, a dreadful explosion of gunpowder took place in a house adjacent to the brewery; eight lives were lost, and great damage done. For a long time it seemed beyond hope to expect to keep the fire from our premises. The morning changed me from affluence to competence, and the evening was likely to have converted competence into poverty. To finish all at night my house was robbed....Yet I find that I can suffer my own misfortunes with comparative indifference, but cannot so easily sit under the misfortunes of those that are near to me.

As was common in those times and, perhaps helped by the habit of all the Earlham girls including Hannah of keeping introspective diaries, he often wrote self-critical memoranda, examining himself and his motives and principles. He did not keep a diary, but his Memoranda Books contain many such introspective records. This had been a widespread custom and those biographers who misunderstand it as undue morbidity and self-doubt fail to see its merit. If to us they may appear unduly self-critical, so that some biographers accuse their authors of being neurotic, they had many merits. They were a good defence against conceit, selfish motives and the desire for reputation. Certainly Buxton found it so. Mottram, in his biography[7], and others writing about the evangelical philanthropists of the period, fail to understand this. They often cannot understand how the introspective piety of these people resulted quite logically in practical and often costly service well above the level of any religion of mere duty. It produced a powerful motive of gratefulness for obeying God and serving mankind.

One of the best examples comes from January 1817 when he is writing to his wife from London after visiting some condemned prisoners in Newgate Gaol:

> It has made me long much that my life may not pass quite uselessly; but that, in some shape or other, I may assist in checking and diminishing crime and its consequent misery. Surely it is in the power of all to do something in the service of their Master; and surely I among the rest, if I were now to begin and endeavour, to the best of my capacity, to serve Him, might be the means of good to some of my fellow-creatures.
>
> This capacity is, I feel, no mean talent, and attended with no inconsiderable responsibility. I must pray that I may at length stir myself up, and be enabled to feel somewhat of the real spirit of a missionary, and that I may devote myself, my influence, my time, and above all, my affections, to the honour of God, and the happiness of man.
>
> My mission is evidently not abroad, but it is no less a mission on that account. I feel that I may journey through life by two very different paths, and that the time is now come for choosing which I will pursue. I may go on, as I have been going on, not absolutely neglectful of futurity, nor absolutely devoted to it. I may get riches and repute,

and gratify my ambition, and do some good and more evil: and, at length, I shall find all my time on earth expended, and in retracing my life I shall see little but occasions lost, and capabilities misapplied. The other is a path of more labour and less indulgence. I may become a real soldier of Christ; I may feel that I have no business on earth but to do his will and to walk in his ways, and I may direct every energy I have to the service of others. Of these paths, I know which I would most gladly choose: 'but what I would, that I do not; but what I hate, that I do'.

At the start of each year he gave time to a critical review of the past year, thanksgiving for good received and concern to do better in the year ahead, frequently ending with a list of practical priorities for the year ahead. Thus on Jan. lst, 1932, in the middle of the final battle for liberation, he wrote:

> O Lord, how much have I had in the past year to thank thee for! What mercy, what love, what compassion for my weakness, what readiness to pardon....
>
> Now, am I sufficiently assiduous in the discharge of my duties? My great duty is the deliverance of my brethren in the West Indies from slavery both of body and soul. In the early part of the year I did in some measure faithfully discharge this.... but, latterly, where has my heart been? Has the bondage of my brethren engrossed my whole mind? The plain and painful fact is that it has not. Pardon, O Lord, this neglect of the honourable service to which thou hast called me. Give me wisdom to devise, and ability to execute, and zeal and perseverance and dedication of heart, for the task with which thou hast been pleased to honour me.
> 2 Chron.20.12-17.

Like most others with an evangelical faith he could face up to his faults, because he had confidence that they could be forgiven. To many other people it is too painful and this sort of introspection seems unreal. Buxton could explore the worst in his life because he could be sure of the best in God's mercy.

Social and Religious Concerns

Between 1813 and 1816 his 'common place books' are chiefly filled with memoranda on various charitable subjects with which he was increasingly becoming involved. In the absence of serious

The Brewery of Hanbury and Buxton in Brick Lane, East London. The Buxtons lived there, until in 1815 they moved with their three children to the more healthy Hampstead.

public medical services for the poor, he and some relatives became involved in helping the main hospital in the area – The London Hospital.[8] By 1815 he had so far completed the reorganisation of the business that he could make more spare time, leaving much of the day to day work to others. In fact the business, and some financial help from his mother, provided him with a more than adequate income for the rest of his life, without requiring his daily attention at Brick Lane. He also moved house in 1815 to Hampstead to provide a more healthy situation for the growing family of four children and to be near his brother-in-law Samuel Hoare, with whom he shared many charitable concerns. London's East End was notoriously unhealthy and was soon to suffer large scale cholera epidemics. Charles Simeon who stayed with them in Hampstead wrote to J.J. Gurney: 'More of heaven I never saw than in the two families in Hampstead'.[9] When in 1817 his remaining brother Charles died aged 33, Buxton bought a house in Hampstead for the widow and her three children, forming a very happy family group. Amongst others Thomas Chalmers, the Scottish evangelical leader, who shared an active concern for the poor and had led the way in Scotland, stayed with them.

His education project in Spitalfields was proving effective. He was no intellectual or social snob, and writing to his wife in 1815 he says:

> I went this evening to a general meeting of the adult school... The good that has already been done is, is quite extraordinary: exclusive of one hundred and fifty persons who have improved in reading, eighty nine, who did not know their letters can now read well. We had five exhibited, and their performance was grand; but the effect on their lives is still better than the effect on their literature. Then we had a variety of fine speeches. I do not much admire meetings of ladies and gentlemen, but the tradesmen speaking to the mechanics, is a treat to me: one fine fellow harvested a rich crop of corn off a majestic oak, and the simile was received with a burst of applause. But if this is entertaining, the zeal and warmth with which they speak and act, is very interesting: I really prefer their blundering heartiness, to the cool and chaste performances of more erudite orators.

The winter of 1816 was particularly severe and very little work was available in the neighbourhood of the brewery or throughout the East End. There was great misery and near starvation, with hardly any relief available apart from one inadequate soup kitchen. With Samuel Hoare he set up a committee to find ways of relieving the poor and a public meeting was arranged in the Mansion House to raise a subscription. Buxton was the main speaker and in spite of his own doubts about it the speech was evidently an outstanding success. It was extensively reported in the papers with great favour and congratulations poured in. It was even reprinted by the Government's democratic opposition as 'the best statement of the miseries permitted under the present government' and then by the government's supporters 'because it forms so beautiful a contrast to the language of those wretched demagogues, whose infamous doctrines would increase the evils they affect to deplore'. Political debate does not seem to have changed a lot! Over £43,000 was raised immediately and the Prince Regent (to become George the Fourth in 1820) sent another £5,000 a few days later when he read it. These were very large sums by today's standards. He was beginning to be a figure in public life and he started to think seriously about entering Parliament.

Amongst the letters he received was one from the famous and still active William Wilberforce, who wrote very encouragingly and clearly with purpose:

> My dear sir, I must in three words express the real pleasure, with which I have read and heard, of your successful effort on Tuesday last, in behalf of the hungry and the naked. But I cannot claim that the merit of being influenced only by regard for the Spitalfields' sufferers.... It is partly a selfish feeling, for I anticipate the success of the efforts, which I trust you will one day make in other instances, in an assembly in which I trust we shall one day be fellow-labourers, both in the motives by which we are activated, and in the objects to which our exertions will be directed. I am dear Sir,
> Yours sincerely, W Wilberforce

Prison Reform and Elizabeth Fry

His sister-in-law Elizabeth Fry[10] had since 1813 been interested in relieving the miseries of prisoners in Newgate Prison. Her attention had been drawn to this by an American Quaker of French extraction who, while stopping off with her on a preaching tour had visited some French prisoners of war. He was horrified by what he saw and Elizabeth immediately set about trying to meet some of the physical needs of the prisoners. It seems however that, probably because of her frequent pregnancies (ten children in sixteen years) and a restricted financial position of her husband, whose business suffered some serious setbacks, she did little more for the time being. In 1814, 1815 and 1816 however Sam Hoare and Buxton invited her to join them in visits to various prisons in London and by 1817 she was launched into a major programme of help to the women prisoners, whose condition was almost unbelievably horrible. A crowd of women were herded like animals into a small space with their almost naked children sleeping on the bare floor. Men prisoners were allowed into the women's quarters at night and there was much drunkenness, immorality and fighting. Elizabeth was warned not to wear her watch when she went in or it would certainly be snatched off her. She refused to comply and had a remarkable effect in calming the wild confusion of the place.

The two men had already launched with others in 1816 'The Society for the Reformation of Prison Discipline' and had achieved a few changes, but they were minor and Elizabeth was a determined woman. She started a school for the children of the women, teaching them to read and to count. Almost immediately she was besieged with requests to do the same for the adults. She wanted to give them useful employment and so also to earn a little honest money. She persevered against great odds and even the discouragement of Buxton and Sam Hoare who thought her plans impracticable. She therefore created a committee of well-to-do women to help her. Before long she had it all organised and the women prisoners were taught to sew and knit while she read aloud to them from the Bible, with a short exhortation.

Buxton was involved in helping her to organise the sale of the products and probably in other expenses. The spectacle of her reading to those who shortly before had been regarded as totally out of control, while they worked quietly, was something to visit and led her into a very influential role in prison reform, not only in Britain, but overseas. Letters seeking her advice poured in from many countries. The French Ambassador wrote home saying that he had now seen the two greatest sights in London: St Paul's Cathedral and Mrs Fry reading to the prisoners in Newgate.[11]

Elizabeth was, especially for her time, a truly remarkable woman. Few women had been able to take such a public role and push through their initiatives as she did. She was ahead of her time also in her strategies. She drew the prisoners into all her plans. They chose the prisoners to run the school. She divided the adults into work groups and they chose a 'monitor' for each group learning to sew and to knit and read. They advised her on the needs and methods. With rare exceptions they responded with a discipline that was almost incredible to those who knew the dissolute and uncontrollable reputation of the place.

She was also clever in dealing with the authorities, who steadily opposed her plans at first. In session with the two Sheriffs of London and the Governor of the Prison she pushed them into saying that the chief objection was the lack of space. She then got them to say that that was the only serious objection and went off to the prisoners to get them to clear a room. That was 'Check Mate' and they had to allow her to try.

She visited the convict ships taking prisoners to Australia and found them chaotic, immoral and allowing no employment on the long voyage. She organised sewing classes so that on arrival in Australia they would have something to sell and a skill to use. She visited every convict ship between 1818 and 1843 distributing Bibles and other literature for the journey. Before long she was called to give evidence to a Committee of the House of Commons and went with some trepidation, her brother J.J. Gurney accompanying her to give support. In the event she had her usual perfect confidence and followed it up with visits to the Home Secretary to persuade him to do more. As a result she was soon famous in Britain and respected all over the continent, where she visited to persuade others to improve their prisons. She found herself invited to meet the heads of state and royal families and became a celebrity. She was criticised for neglecting her large family and was perhaps more respected and admired than loved by those of her own class. When her husband went bankrupt and was therefore 'disowned' by the Quakers she was put in a difficult position, but stayed a strict Quaker and minister. What she achieved was quite outstanding. She was able also to supply Buxton with all the details that he needed for his speeches in Parliament on the convict ships and the prisons.

Buxton, however, while he helped Elizabeth Fry's efforts financially, set himself rather to try to change the law and the public opinion that had made such things possible. On a visit to France to try to set up a branch of the Bible Society in Paris, he visited several French prisons. As a result he was asked to write up an account of the French prison system. As he said : this 'work grew insensibly upon my hands' into a more wide ranging treatment of the prisons.

At the end of 1817 he set down his personal priorities for the New Year as:

> To write a pamphlet on Prison Discipline.
> To establish a Savings Bank in Spitalfields.
> To recommence the sale of salt fish in Spitalfields.
> To attend to the London Hospital, and to endeavour to make the clergyman perform his duties, or get him superseded.
> To establish a new Bible Association.

He added: 'May the grace of God assist me in these objects; may he sanctify my motives, and guard me from pride, and may I use my utmost exertions, making his will mine.' This last note comes often in his writing. He was always conscious of the danger of wrong motives creeping into his public actions.

By now he was spending time helping the Bible Society and taking an interest in helping and speaking for the Church Missionary Society, which was another of his lifelong concerns. He was also in consultation with the Bishop of London about the acute needs of the poor in the city and with others about the needs that led in 1834 to the creation of the London City Mission, with its combination of evangelism and relief. When that Mission was created in 1834 he was its first Treasurer.

At the 1817 election he was invited to consider standing for Weymouth and went down to explore it, but decided against. He wrote: 'I am far from regretting that I came, as I do not doubt that it will secure an independent seat at the next election. That word 'independent' has been the obstacle upon this occasion, and I hope to spend the next two years in preparation for the House.'

In Feb. 1818 he finally published his pamphlet: *An inquiry whether crime be produced or prevented by our present System of Prison Discipline*. He argued that it frequently made people worse. It immediately received far more attention than he had anticipated. It ran through six editions in the first year and was referred to with praise in Parliament. It was also noticed abroad and drew a further letter of commendation from William Wilberforce who added:

> May it please God to continue to animate you with as much benevolent zeal, and to direct it to worthy objects. I hope you will soon come into Parliament, and be able to contend in person, as well as with your pen, for the rights of the oppressed and the friendless. I claim you as an ally in this blessed league.

CHAPTER 4

In Parliament

IN 1818 THERE WAS another election and he stood for Weymouth and was duly elected, taking his seat in 1819 on the Tory side with Wilberforce, but still guarding his independence. In future elections he stood as a Whig. In a personal memorandum, after further praying for pure motives he wrote:

> Now that I am a member of Parliament, I feel earnest for the honest, diligent, and conscientious discharge of the duty I have undertaken. My prayer is for the guidance of God's Holy Spirit, that, free from views of gain or popularity, – that, careless of all things but fidelity to my trust, I may be enabled to do some good to my country, and something for mankind, especially in their most important concerns. I feel the responsibility of the situation and its many temptations.

His speaking style had developed by now. He was not a sparkling speaker. His strength was in careful argument and meticulous presentation of evidence, but not without wit and some sarcasm. He studied carefully what kind of speaking was acceptable and effective in the House, writing that the House liked only 'good sense and joking'. He was not good at joking, but excellent at good sense. Wilberforce, who was an orator, said of him: 'he was a man who could hew a statue out of a rock, but not cut faces on cherry stones'. He was clear, forceful and earnest. He took a lot of care in preparing his speeches; not much on finding smart phrases but much on presentation of facts in a line of argument. He could rise to passion about a topic about which he felt strongly, but he was more often businesslike seeking to persuade by reasons.

Buxton and Wilberforce became close collaborators and must have been a remarkable pair when on the same platform as they often were. Wilberforce was only 5 foot 4 inches and his figure was almost twisted. He was described by James Boswell as a 'shrimp', though he added that as he spoke: 'presently the shrimp swelled into a whale'. 'Elephant' Buxton's figure beside him must have seemed almost comical. Wilberforce's speeches were often dramatic. Buxton spoke in a more closely argued way, but they enjoyed an identity of Christian faith, of aims in life and as parliamentarians, as well as a very warm friendship. Buxton once wrote, rather surprisingly: 'I think it odd that we should suit so well, having hardly one quality in common'. Wilberforce was now almost 60 and his health and eyesight were beginning to fail. He also had serious family worries and some considerable financial problems created by one of his sons, which prevented his living near to Parliament any longer. As a result he could not often manage the frequent late night sessions.

Entering the House of Commons Buxton found himself with a number of people who had similar interests to his own. There were several older stalwarts of the Slave Trade battles, including Wilberforce, Thomas Babington and Dr Stephen Lushington[1], and several personal friends, a few of whom were ex-Quakers like his wife's cousin Robert Gurney. There were still no Quaker MPs. Dissenters were only allowed after 1828.

Wilberforce had proposed a Bill for a very mild penal reform in 1786 and, although it had been passed in the Commons, the Lords had defeated it, as they still had the power summarily to defeat Commons legislation. The subject had then received little attention as the Slave Trade issue and the war with France had pushed it to one side. In 1819 Wilberforce raised the issue again by presenting a petition from the Quakers, but when asked if he planned to bring forward legislation himself he replied that this was now beyond his powers. He said 'I can write but little, I can scarcely read at all'. In his speech he called for 'some individual of competent knowledge, industry and ability' to do so.

Recent legislation had increased the number of capital offences enormously. Buxton counted 230 offences punishable by death and there seemed to be an assumption that the only way to tackle crime was to apply more and more ferocious penalties.[2] There were public hangings after every local Assize and they included quite young people who had stolen trifles. Buxton wrote that if he could only remove forgery, sheep stealing and horse stealing from the list he could save at least 30 lives a year.

Early in 1819, soon after he had entered Parliament, Buxton took part in three debates on the state of the convict ships that were taking prisoners to Australia. He wrote to J.J. Gurney on February 25th:

> When I last spoke (on the state of the convict ships) there was....marked attention: but alas, most undeserved, for, like a blockhead, I rose, having nothing to say, and without a moment's premeditation. This has mortified me, which proves that my motives are not purified from selfish desires for reputation. I despise this vanity. On Monday next, comes on the question of prisons: on Tuesday, the question of the penal code. On the latter I shall speak with my arguments and facts clearly before me. If I then fail, the failure is final – I may serve the cause as a labourer, but neither this, nor any other, as an advocate.

On March 1st Lord Castlereagh, one of the many sons of Peers who held seats in the House of Commons that were more or less controlled by their fathers, carried a motion for a committee to enquire into the state of prison discipline. On the next evening Sir James Mackintosh[3] proposed a committee on the criminal laws. Buxton seconded the latter in his first carefully prepared parliamentary speech and it was evidently a considerable success. That encouraged him greatly. Clearly he had learned from his earlier failure. He wrote again to J.J. Gurney:

> I spoke for nearly an hour. I was low and dispirited, and much tired (bodily) when I rose. I cannot say I pleased myself. I could not at first get that freedom of language, that is so essential, but I rose with the cheers of the House, and contrived to give much of what was on my mind. Everybody seems to have taken a more favourable opinion of the speech than I did. The facts were irresistible: and, for fear of tiring my auditors, I confined myself principally to facts. You will see by the papers that we obtained a victory. As for myself, I hope I did force myself into something like indifference to my own success, provided the cause succeeded.

It was a very good start to his future standing as a debater in the House. One MP commented: 'Buxton acquitted himself to universal satisfaction. The House is prepared to receive him with respect and kindness: and his sterling sense, his good language, and his earnest manner, fully keep up the preposition in his favour, so that I recollect very few who have made their debut with so much advantage.' Buxton found himself appointed as a member of both the select committees concerned.

He states that he was probably the only member of the committee on the penal code who wished the death penalty abolished on all offences except murder. While he believed in just punishment he believed that the code and the prisons should *also* aim to rehabilitate criminals and return them as useful members of society. He was giving Elizabeth Fry financial help to teach prisoners trades that might earn them some money when they were in prison and when they were discharged. At the first meeting of the committee that was preparing a Prison Bill he put forward a well prepared set of proposals for their work and almost all of these were soon adopted. That committee quickly presented a Bill that was passed without difficulty and resulted in some improvements.

To an old TCD friend, John Henry North, whom he was trying to persuade to join him in Parliament, (successfully in the end) he wrote in that same year:

> I care little about party politics. I vote as I like: sometimes pro and sometimes con; but I feel the greatest interest in subjects such as the Slave Trade (i.e. at this stage getting other nations to ban it and maintaining the naval squadron on the West African coast to police it), the condition of the poor, prisons and criminal law... I am on the Jail and criminal law Committees and devote three mornings a week to one and three to the other: so I am contented, and feel as little inclination, as ability, to engage in political contentions.

At the start of 1820 he again lists his priorities. Putting the criminal code and prisons first, he adds that he wants to attack 'Suttee' in India and raise funds for Sunday Schools in Spitalfields, though his health again limited what he could do for several months. Because of the death of the King (George the Third) there was another election in 1820 and at first he hesitated about standing again, partly because he now had eight children and of course a job in the brewery. He did however stand and was again elected for Weymouth stating that he hoped do be able to do more for the disadvantaged. A delightful and very warm letter from Charles Simeon of Cambridge warns him of the danger of being seen as a Radical if he identified with their programmes. This was probably because any reformers were liable to be called 'Jacobins' by conservatives and suspected of sympathies with the French Revolution. The radical protests that were taking place in England were often identified with it in the public mind as some of the leaders, and Irish nationalists like Robert Emmett were influenced by it. It had tended to produce a strong conservative reaction.

Wilberforce had been the target of ferocious and often quite unfair criticisms by Cobbett and others on the radical side. It was also true that Clarkson, who had done so much to collect and circulate information on the Slave Trade and was still active in that, had at least at first openly supported the French Revolution, to the acute embarrassment of Wilberforce and the whole movement. Buxton, however, was his own man and sometimes offended his supporters by his open support of causes that they could not agree. His warm friendship with Wilberforce did not mean that he was uncritical of the great man. He remarked that Wilberforce was by that time liable to lose his train of thought in debate. Wilberforce was also more strongly conservative than Buxton, perhaps partly because of his strong friendship with Pitt, though Pitt was not very conservative, and, after he died in 1806, Wilberforce seemed to be more of a Whig. Both Wilberforce and Buxton were attacked in their time from the right for being Radicals in disguise and from the left for being hypocritical defenders of the status quo at home. Like many others they were genuinely fearful of revolution in Britain and felt that the authorities needed support.

1819 was the year of the 'Peterloo Massacre' when the militia were called out by extremely nervous magistrates (there was no proper civilian police force yet) to deal with a peaceful demonstration by 50,000 cotton operatives. A vicious charge by sabre wielding horsemen had resulted in 11 deaths and hundreds wounded. Buxton did not speak in the Peterloo debate but wrote: 'I voted with the ministers, because I cannot bring myself to subject the Manchester magistrates to a parliamentary enquiry, but nothing has shaken my convictions that the magistrates, ministers and all, have done exceeding wrong'. Nevertheless Buxton was now clearly a Whig, was elected as a Whig and sat with them on the opposition benches.

At this point domestic disaster struck. In April 1820 his eldest son, aged 10, was sent home from school sick and died suddenly. Then his three youngest girls, aged 4, 3 and 1½ contracted whooping cough followed by measles and all died within a few weeks. He was a devoted family man and he was very deeply hurt. He always enjoyed fun with his children and had been in the habit of playing games with the girls, buying little presents to hide in the house for them to find and allowing them to interrupt his work with trivial requests, however busy he was. His wife was shattered and needed a lot of support. Coming back to the house and finding the three little hats still hanging on their pegs was too much, and she could not settle in the house again. They withdrew to the country for a year with, as he put it, 'the fragments of our family' and then moved again, this time to Hannah's beloved Norfolk, where near Cromer she had happy memories of holidays with Gurney relatives. Here they rented Cromer Hall from friends until they moved in 1828 into nearby Northrepps Hall. Although they were more than one day's journey by Mail Coach from London the move was permanent. He no longer needed to spend so much time at the brewery and he could work and read uninterrupted on his parliamentary business when he was not in London, where he kept a working base near to Parliament and did some parliamentary letter writing from the brewery when he was there.

He loved the country, purchased land nearby and delighted in planting trees and in country sports. Fortunately his Norfolk Gamekeeper, Larry Banville, kept a diary. These have been edited and published recently.[4] With occasional grumbles Banville described Buxton at one time as 'his earthly father in Norfolk'. He obviously held him in great regard and said of him that probably 'there would not be a better master in the kingdom'. Buxton's sons treated Banville as a friend, Charles signing a letter to Banville from London as 'Your friend', though of course the differences of wealth and status were accepted. Northrepps, where again he hired and never owned a house, became a bolt hole from the pressures of Parliament and his not infrequent periods of exhaustion and illness. As he had hoped it also proved more healthy for the family. He befriended the local farm labourers and fishermen, inviting them to share the prayers which he conducted daily when he was there. He was generous and much loved and respected locally. When buying a joint of pork from a cottager, who had fallen on hard times and needed to sell, he paid for another for the man himself, saying that it was a shame for the man not to have part of his own pig! He successfully cured the Gamekeeper of excessive drinking by lending him a gun, which would become a gift if he kept off drink for a sufficient period.

By 1820 however, Buxton was back in action and extremely busy. He speaks of working 'very, very hard'. He had discussions with the police and with Elizabeth Fry and others interested in the prisons. He was also involved in *The African Institution*. This was a body set up by Wilberforce and his colleagues a few weeks after the passing of the 1807 Act abolishing the British Trade. It had become totally preoccupied with persuading other countries to stop their Trade also, and to ensure that the Act was enforced on British ships and as far as was possible on ships of other countries. It seems that it had become a little sleepy. Buxton cancelled some shooting to attend a meeting! Unexpectedly he felt compelled to speak and to reprimand them for recent inactivity. He feared that he had offended Wilberforce, but, on the contrary, Wilberforce thanked him profusely for stirring things up again.

He wrote to his wife in 1821, apparently from Wilberforce's working base in Palace Yard, describing his past week:

> My hands are rather full: Thursday, Brick Lane. Friday, Cape of Good Hope Slave Trade. Saturday, Lord Lansdowne's [presumably Slavery business. Lansdowne was prominent in the African Institution]. Monday, Prison Bill. Tuesday, Brougham's Bill on Education. Wednesday, I make a speech to the children in Spitalfields. Thursday, Brick Lane and Mail Coach. Friday home. I want two heads, two bodies, and the power of being in two places at once.

His youngest sister-in-law, Priscilla Gurney, had become ill with tuberculosis so he brought her to Cromer, which had a reputation for good health, hoping that that would lead to recovery. She died there, however, a few months later aged 36, but had asked him to come from London to receive her last wish, which was that he would do something about the slaves.

He was however caught up again in the penal code issues and its first result was a Bill for the abolition of the death penalty for forgery. His speech on this (May 23rd, 1821) is worth some quotations to show his style. He set out to prove that the law as it stood was both inhuman and ineffective – ineffective because juries refused to find people guilty under so draconian a law. The result was that guilty people went free to offend again, the law came into contempt and juries clearly perjured themselves. In the course of the speech he said: 'I have in my hand 1200 cases of such perjury'. He left nothing to guesswork. He said:

> We have gone on long enough taking it for granted that capital punishment does restrain crime, and the time is now arrived when we may fairly ask 'Does it do so?'. We have tried nothing else for the last century; and we have tried it on a scale large enough. The law of England has displayed no unnecessary nicety in apportioning the penalty of death; kill your father or a rabbit in warren, the penalty is the same! Destroy three kingdoms or a hopvine, the penalty is the same. Meet a gipsy on the high road, keep company with him, or kill him, the penalty by law is the same!
>
> The system then having been tried long enough, and largely enough, what are the results? Has your law done that which you expected from your law? Has crime decreased? Has it remained stationary? Certainly not. Has it increased? It certainly has, and at a prodigious rate! Why then your system has failed.

Crime, he then reminded them, had in fact increased fourfold in twelve years. Only one experimental fact had been brought forward on the other side. In the case of larceny from the person, mitigation had been tried and conviction for that crime had increased. But then every other crime had increased in an equal or greater ratio. No more had been gained by maintaining capital punishment than by removing it.

> We have done as well without as with the capital punishment. That is our case is proved. To inflict death needlessly, can be called by no other name than that of legal murder.

Now, at the same period, two experiments were tried. In the one case we proceeded from lenity to rigour; in the other, from rigour to lenity Here, then principle is opposed to principle, system to system, and the result is before us. First, in 1807, forgery of stamps was made a capital crime. And the question is, with what effect? The solicitor of the excise declared the change to be a change for the worse: that the excise was better protected by your former lenity than by your late rigour.

But another experiment was tried, very different in its nature and (I rejoice to say) as different in its effects. In 1811 the linen bleachers came to Parliament ... praying for a mitigation in the law against stealing from bleaching grounds. That prayer was conceded; in this House cheerfully. In another place [i.e. the House of Lords] acquiescence was granted somewhat in the same spirit in which the satirist describes the deities of old as yielding to the foolish importunities of their votaries. *Evertere domos totas optantibus ipsis Di faciles.*[5]

And here it was determined to punish these romantic petitioners with the fulfilment of their prayer, and to inflict upon them the penalty of conceded wishes. With what effect?....To answer this question, I will enter into a comparison of which no man will deny the fairness. I will take the last five years during which the crime was capital – and the last five years during which it has not been capital. Now, if I prove that this offence has increased but only in the same proportion with other offences, I prove my point for reasons which I have already assigned. But if I go a step farther, and prove that, while all other offences have increased with the most melancholy rapidity, this, and this alone, has decreased as rapidly, that there is one only exception to the universal augmentation of crime, and that one exception is in the case in which you have reduced the penalty of your law, if I can do this, and upon evidence that cannot be shaken, have I not a right to call upon the noble Lord opposite, and upon his majesty's ministers, either to invalidate my facts, or to admit my conclusion?

He then read from the official returns of crimes committed in the Duchy of Lancaster, showing that whereas since the mitigation of this law all other offences had increased greatly – in the case of stealing from homes eleven fold – stealing from the bleaching yards had decreased by two-thirds. He then referred to the effects of making forgery a capital offence with a nice touch of sarcasm:

> every wretch who was overtaken by the law.... was consigned to the hangman. You accomplished your object no doubt! By dint of such hardness you exterminated the offence as well as the offenders: forgeries of course ceased in a country under such a terrible method of repressing them! No! but they grew, they multiplied, they increased to so enormous an extent that you were absolutely compelled to mitigate your law, because of the multitude of offenders – public feeling, and the feeling of the advisors of the crown, rebelled against such continual slaughter.

He then referred to past history and to what was the situation in other countries, and defended himself against any charge that he was going against the Common Law. On the contrary these numerous capital offences were nearly all recent innovations. He was defending the Common Law against novelties. The present position was resulting in the perjuring of juries and witnesses in order to save lives and the freedom of dangerous criminals etc.

There were numerous expressions of appreciation. Denman, whose critical opinion was worth hearing, remarked that: 'more of wisdom, more of benevolence, more of practical demonstration he had never heard in the course of (his) parliamentary career'.

The motion was, however, narrowly defeated and it had to wait for Robert Peel to become Home Secretary in 1822 for the whole criminal code to be reviewed with acts passed in the following years. This debate however, and the work of the Committees on which Buxton sat, had contributed greatly to the result. The historian, Asa Briggs, comments that the 'committee of 1819, the result of the work of Romilly, Sir James Mackintosh and Thomas Fowell Buxton, had laid the foundations for a major revision'.[6] A growing opinion in favour of revision was being created. It was not long before many offences were removed from that horrendous list. Buxton had to learn that to be defeated did not mean that the cause was lost, or that you should give up. Sometimes it was later to prove that a defeat could be the prelude to an increased awareness in the public mind and in Parliament that something had to be done to tackle an evil. Thankfully, like Wilberforce, he was a very persistent man, whose Christian faith gave him the determination to carry on until undoubted evils were dealt with, even if it made him unpopular.

This tenacity of purpose in the nineteenth century evangelical social reformers is sometimes misunderstood as a guilt driven attempt to make up for their faults and so earn a better place in God's estimate and in heaven. Evangelicals however, if they are consistent, know that that is impossible. These reformers nearly all had a clear knowledge that all is of grace and free gift and that their task is to respond in gratefulness to the mercy and love of God with enthusiastic obedience, including practical service to others. Certainly the diaries of several of them show this perfectly clearly,[7] as Buxton's memoranda certainly do. Some authors have written without reading these personal reflections carefully.

In the circumstances it is not surprising that Buxton hesitated to take over from Wilberforce the campaign for the liberation of the slaves. He had other important concerns running and he could see that the liberation campaign would be very difficult and probably very long term. At least 50 MPs had big financial interests in slavery in the West Indies, and there was a comparable number in the House of Lords. They were referred to as the 'West Indians' and no government without a big majority, which was rare, could afford to offend so many.

CHAPTER 5

The Liberation Cause Adopted

THE DAY AFTER THE debate on the criminal law (May 24th 1821) Buxton received a long letter from Wilberforce urging him to take up the matter of the slaves. Wilberforce repeated his inability now to undertake any long term task and his difficulty in attending the House regularly, especially for late night sessions. He states that:

> For many, many years, I have been longing to bring forward that great subject, the condition of the Negro slaves in our Trans-Atlantic colonies, and the best means of providing for their moral and social improvement and ultimately their advancement to the rank of a free peasantry.....I have been waiting, with no little solicitude, for a proper time and suitable circumstances of the country, for introducing this great business; and, latterly, for some member of Parliament, who, if I were to retire or be laid by, would be an eligible leader of this holy enterprise.
>
> I have for some time been viewing you in this connection; and after what passed last night, I can no longer forbear resorting to you, as I formerly did to Pitt, and earnestly conjuring you to take most seriously into consideration, the expediency of your devoting yourself to this *blessed service*, so far as may be consistent with the due discharge of the obligations you have already contracted. Let me entreat you to form an alliance with me, that may be truly termed holy, and if I should be unable to commence the war (certainly not to be declared this session); and still more, if, when commenced, I should, (as certainly would, I fear, be the case,) be unable to finish it, I do entreat that you would continue to prosecute it.

A year and a half passed without decision, but Buxton spent time reading round the subject. His sister's husband, Mr William Forster (a Quaker 'minister'), Joseph John Gurney and others encouraged him to take it on. Priscilla Gurney's dying wish evidently weighed with him also. He was anxious lest the knowledge of proceedings towards liberation should provoke an insurrection amongst the slaves, as its opponents often predicted. He wrote: 'If a servile war should break out, and 50,000 perish, how should I like that?'. Finally Wilberforce with Lushington and Zachary Macaulay, all of them veterans of the Slave Trade battles, came to Cromer for a full discussion. They were joined by Lord Suffield, a Norfolk neighbour and landowner, who was to be an important advocate in the House of Lords and outside it.[1] Perhaps prompted by Wilberforce's obviously failing health, Buxton agreed in October 1822. Shortly afterwards Wilberforce wrote:

> My dear Buxton, my remorse is sometimes very great, from my consciousness, that we have not been duly active in endeavouring to put an end to that system of cruel bondage, which for two centuries has prevailed in our West Indian Colonies; and my idea is, that, a little before Parliament meets, three or four of us should have a secret council, wherein we should deliberate to decide what course to pursue.

Buxton and Macaulay met often at Wilberforce's home at Marden Park (15 miles from Parliament, now that he could no longer afford to live in Westminster).

As he contemplated a new session of Parliament, Buxton wrote in his 'common-place' book:

> Let me then never pass a day without serious and repeated prayer – that is indispensable. Let me renounce the world as much as possible; as much as possible acknowledge God in all my ways and words, and let me manfully resist every temptation, which may endanger my soul. O God, grant these things through thy blessed Son! Next, how can I promote the welfare of others? In private, by more seriousness in family devotions, and by much more command of temper; by more industry; by more economy, sparing my own pleasure and expending on God's service. In public, by attending to the Slave Trade, Slavery, Indian widows

burning themselves, the completion of those objects which have made some advance, viz. Criminal Law, Prisons, and Police.

This is a good example of how his priorities worked. The subjective concern with his spiritual state and progress was quite naturally linked to very practical outworking in a variety of philanthropic activities. There is no trace of a tension between the two such as sometimes seems to have arisen in the twentieth century.

Buxton's Team

Buxton was far from alone in the campaign. In Parliament he had the invaluable support and advice of Wilberforce for a few more years, of Dr Lushington, and Sir James Mackintosh. There was Lord Suffield, leading in the House of Lords and others in both Houses who had supported the abolition of the Trade and were willing, in some cases rather cautiously, to support liberation if it could be presented as no attack on private property. That was an extremely sensitive issue so that liberation did not follow automatically from the abolition of the Trade in the minds of many people. They had been joined by some newer MPs, notably Thomas Denman, who had become an MP in 1819. He was a gracious and warm friend. It was said of him that 'he was beloved of all who knew him'.[2] There was also Henry Brougham, who had been active in the matter of slavery outside Parliament before he became an MP in 1810, but was a cold and devastating speaker and loved by very few. He is described as 'a bitter enemy and a jealous colleague'.[3] His sharp features matched his acerbic wit.

The older circle around Wiberforce who had fought for abolition and for a number of other moral and social causes are today often referred to as the 'Clapham Sect' or ' the men of Clapham'. They were of course never a sect in any sense, but several of them lived on Clapham Common and others used to come and stay there to plan their initiatives, supported by the Vicar of Clapham, John Venn.[4] They had worked at the revision of the charter of the East India Company to allow education and missionary work in India, the founding of the Bible Society and the Church Missionary Society, Sunday observance, and attacked duelling and the lottery and promoted education and Sunday Schools. They were behind the founding of Sierra Leone and various other societies such as the Society for the Reformation of Manners. During their lifetime they were often caustically referred to as 'The Saints' and it was only in 1844 that they began to be called the Clapham Sect after the grandson of one of them had given them the title.[5] The best description of them would be 'a brotherhood of evangelical social reformers'. By no means all of them were in Parliament but all were working for political and social change. Some key members were MPs, notably Wilberforce, Henry Thornton,[6] who died in 1815, Thomas Babington of Rothley Temple, Charles Grant and John Shore (later Lord Teignmouth). The last two had special knowledge of India, Shore having been Governor General of India, and Grant a Director of the East India Company. Both men had the fine reputation, amongst people involved with India, of being men of total integrity and honesty.

That generation, however, with notable exceptions had either died or become less active through ill health when Buxton became leader of the younger parliamentary group pushing for similar reforms. Buxton and his allies were the parliamentary heirs of Wilberforce and his generation, but not really part of the 'Clapham Sect', though they are sometimes referred to in those terms. Certainly they had the same motivation and religious basis.

Outside Parliament Buxton had a group of devoted workers led by Thomas Clarkson and Zachary Macaulay. Both had played a very important part in collecting and presenting relevant information and arousing public concern on the Trade. They now turned their energies to the question of slavery itself. Clarkson, now fully recovered from his 'breakdown', had married a splendid lady, who proved to be a fine partner and fresh inspiration. He had moved back to nearer London and now emerged again as a tireless worker, touring the country to arouse concern over the liberation issue and still busy in attempts to persuade other countries to abolish the Trade. Buxton frequently gave him credit for his role and Wordsworth wrote a Sonnet: 'To Thomas Clarkson' to celebrate his work.

Zachary Macaulay (1768-1836) was a rather dour Scot, the son of a Presbyterian minister, who had gone out to the West Indies aged 16 as a clerk on an estate. He was intensely angered by what he saw at first hand. He came home and visited his sister who was married to the evangelical MP, Thomas Babington of Rothley Temple in Leicestershire. Here he experienced a profound religious change through the Babingtons and Rothley Temple became a resort of the group who were battling together against the Trade. There is also a small monument there to mark the meeting between Babington and Wilberforce to draw up motions for Parliament on the Trade. Macaulay was asked to collect more information on the Trade, went out to Sierra Leone and daringly took a passage on a slaver to see what it was really like before becoming Governor of the settlement. He was a very able man, a Fellow of the Royal Society, a keen educationalist along the lines of Bell and Lancaster and one of the founders of University College, London. Much of his writing was anonymous 'for better effect'. In 1802 he had become editor of *The Christian Observer* for 14 years which gave him a big readership. He had an astonishing ability to remember, collect and classify information. When in doubt about relevant information it was common for the others to say 'Let us look it up in Macaulay!' as if he was an encyclopaedia. He was extremely accurate and local supporters were told: 'whatever Macaulay says can be taken for gospel and quoted'. On the passing of the Liberation Act Buxton wrote to him: 'My sober and deliberate opinion is, that you have done more towards this consummation than any other man'. Buxton called him 'the anti-slavery tutor of us all'. Without these two Buxton could not have done what he did.

There was also James Stephen the elder (1758-1832), a Scottish lawyer, who came back from a spell of work in the West Indies 'burning with indignation' at what he had seen, including the burning alive of a slave as a punishment. He became a lawyer of note, and Master in Chancery. He was an important legal adviser, for a short while an active MP after 1808, and a very good speaker in and out of Parliament. He became Wilberforce's brother in law, marrying Wilberforce's widowed sister. Like Macaulay he wrote very well and was described as 'the ablest pamphleteer of his day'. He was a consistent fighter for the cause, though at times quite explosive in his anger at the hindrances and procrastinations of the government. Macaulay and James Stephen were described as 'the authors-general of our cause'.[7] These had all been active in helping to defeat the Slave Trade. Buxton himself never went to the West Indies, indeed when he proposed doing so he was warned not to, because his life would be in very serious danger from the wrath of the planters! These allies and others however gave him plenty of information and fed the public with reliable facts about the gross evils of the system.

Before long the next generation of enthusiastic helpers arose. Thomas Babington Macaulay (Tom), Zachary's son was one. He was later to become Lord Macaulay the historian and literary giant, though at that later stage he lost much of his reforming and Christian zeal. When in 1830 he became an MP he was able to fight alongside Buxton as an important ally. James Stephen's two sons, James and George, were very active in the cause and Lord Glenelg (Charles Grant junior) who became Colonial Secretary. James Stephen junior had important posts at the Colonial Office, becoming Permanent Under-Secretary where he was able to give very important advice as to how to draft motions and memoranda and approach the Government. His power in the Colonial Office became such that he was referred to by some as ' Mr Over-Secretary Stephen'.

In addition, of course, there was the whole network of Quaker families, who were increasingly important in public life. They had usually led the way in agitations about the Trade and were equally committed to the cause of liberation. In fact many of them had been pressing for liberation from the start, even when Wilberforce was hanging fire in order to get the Trade ended. They drew in people of all sorts of Christian background into local committees and activities. John Wesley had written against slavery and therefore many Methodists were easily involved locally in meetings and distribution of literature. The Free Churches included relatively few members who had the vote as yet, but were becoming an important force. Local activities however, absolutely depended upon plenty of reliable information and that was what Clarkson and Macaulay provided in frequent briefings and in Macaulay's writings.

Finally there were a number of his own and his wife's relatives who gave invaluable help. His brothers-in-law Samuel Hoare, William Forster, and Joseph John Gurney supported and encouraged him all through and spoke alongside him in public meetings. There were also two very special women, always referred to as the 'Cottage Ladies'; his unmarried sister, Sarah Maria Buxton, and a cousin of his wife's, Anna Gurney, from Keswick Hall, who lived together in Northrepps Cottage, near to Buxton's Norfolk base. At a time when there were no parliamentary secretaries they did trojan work for him. Especially when he was ill or discouraged these family friends were invaluable.

Sierra Leone

Following Lord Mansfield's judgement in 1772 many slaves in Britain claimed their freedom but the result was not altogether happy. Many owners of slaves refused to employ them now at a wage. London especially saw hundreds of ex-slaves reduced to begging on the streets. A good many were given free passage to Nova Scotia, where they joined other ex-slaves who, because they had fought for the British against USA, had been given freedom there but very little and rather poor land. They found the very cold climate unbearable.

The evangelical philanthropists of the Clapham group, led by Granville Sharp and Thomas Clarkson, first tried to help in London and then, with government financial support, started a West African settlement at Sierra Leone on the west coast of Africa for repatriated slaves. They hoped that it would become a 'Province of Freedom'. In 1787 therefore a party of 400 (230 negro men, 41 negro women with 70 volunteer white women, of whom many turned out to be prostitutes!) was sent from London, but nearly half died within the first year and the rest were subject to attack from local tribes and slavers. The settlement seemed to be a failure.

In 1891 *The Sierra Leone Company* was set up in London to introduce 'trade, industry and Christian knowledge' with Wilberforce, Thomas Clarkson, Granville Sharp and Thomas Babington as directors and Henry Thornton as Chairman.

In the same year the Committee arranged for the remnant at Sierra Leone to be joined by over 1100 of the former USA slaves from Nova Scotia. They were brought over by a naval vessel under the command of Lieutenant John Clarkson, the brother of Thomas. He had been sent to find some volunteers and, recruiting through the churches, everyone was surprised by the response. These were mostly evangelical Christians, who had been touched by the Second Evangelical Awakening in USA, but had not been treated so well as they had expected, since priority was usually given to the white settlers there. To return to their roots in Africa seemed very attractive, and they injected a strongly evangelical element into the Settlement. They marched up from the ship singing hymns and formed the first Church of modern times on African soil. The settlement however still had formidable problems to face before it came to success.

In 1793 Zachary Macaulay was sent out and became superintendent and then in 1794, at the age of only 26, Governor, until 1799. He then came home to be Secretary of the Company until in 1808 it became a Crown Colony under government control. It was the first British Colony in Africa and the new arrivals set up the first African church of modern times. It was not the result of foreign missionary effort.[8] In spite of numerous vicissitudes, including being attacked and largely destroyed by a French squadron during the wars, Sierra Leone played a big part in the whole process of development, education and Christian evangelism in West Africa. Buxton was not involved in the early stages, but was later to be very interested in its development and active in promoting it. Some of the later ideas of Buxton and others such as Livingstone can be traced back to being built on the vision of this difficult experiment.

This was the same year that the Trade was abolished in British areas of control and a Naval task force set up to patrol the West Coast of Africa. Macaulay gained great experience in Sierra Leone as he had to handle the administration, finance and trade and keep careful records for the Committee in London. During his time there Sierra Leone grew into a reasonably prosperous community, though it was never far from trouble in these early days and was attacked several times. Things did not do so well after he left, until 1800 when a party of 550 free Jamaican blacks (maroons) was brought in.[9]

The original committee members continued a strong interest in the progress of the Colony and in Christian education there well after 1808. Captured slave ships were taken there by the Naval patrols and freed slaves were landed, each being given ¼ acre of land to cultivate. By 1825 18,000 slaves had been returned. They were uprooted from many different tribes and animistic beliefs, and progress was slow and difficult until Christian teaching was established and gave a cultural coherence to the community.

The Church Missionary Society took a special interest and sent missionaries, many of whom died of fever. Of the 79 missionaries and teachers sent out by the CMS only 14 remained in the Colony by 1826 owing to death or sickness. The Methodist and Baptist Missionary Societies had the same sort of experience and the place became known as the White Man's Grave. In 1827 Fourah Bay

College was set up in the capital, Freetown, and began more advanced education. Numerous negro teachers and catechists were trained in Sierra Leone and became pioneers in evangelising West Africa. The first student enrolled at Fourah Bay College was Samuel Crowther, a re-captive from a slave ship, and he was to become the first black bishop in tropical Africa, interestingly discovering his mother still alive in what is now Nigeria on one of his journeys. The first two African students sent from Fourah Bay to complete a medical training in Britain, qualified as early as 1858.[10] Others were sent later for other degrees to Durham University, England and graduated from 1879. These were remarkable achievements for the times and show how strongly, and justifiably, this group of reformers believed in the equal ability of Africans.

The Situation in 1822

It was becoming increasingly clear that there was still a great deal of unfinished business on the Trade. Britain had led the way in abolishing it and had actively pursued a policy of trying to persuade other governments to do the same, especially in the treaties after the war with France. Napoleon had actually abolished it officially in France in 1815 probably in an attempt to stop other French Colonies in the West Indies from joining the British or rebelling into independence, but it continued on a considerable scale after the fall of Napoleon. It was not until 1830 that France introduced effective measures. Meanwhile, although Denmark, Sweden and Holland had withdrawn, the big players, Spain and Portugal, continued in spite of British efforts until 1835. Brazil and Cuba had also taken up much of the Trade and they were harder to persuade, continuing until 1852 in Brazil and 1867 in Cuba. There was also a good deal of smuggling of slaves into USA from Spanish territories. No-one knew how big the continuing Trade was, though by 1851 there were estimated to be 6,000,000 slaves in Brazil, many more than in 1800.[11] Illegal Trade continued in many countries after its official abolition.

The British naval squadron on the West African coast tried to arrest ships and return the slaves on board to freedom, chiefly at Sierra Leone. The Navy however, only captured about 1,500 a year and there were convincing accounts of slavers throwing the slaves overboard to the sharks before capture so as to profess that they were not slave ships and avoid seizure. The Trade in fact was going on still on a vast scale and was as ghastly as ever.

If it is asked why Wilberforce and his colleagues did not attack slavery itself from the start, the answer is clearly that, if they had done so, the Trade would not have been abolished so early. The Trade was most obviously horrendous and did not directly touch the question of private property. The agitations leading to its abolition created a world wide conscience about the way less developed peoples were being treated. There had been considerable discussion as to which should be attacked first – slavery or the Trade. Clarkson had argued persuasively that if the Trade was stopped then slavery would die of itself. He had proved too optimistic and now changed his view, even on one occasion charging Wilberforce with delaying the liberation of the slaves. Property owners thought that the abolition of the Trade would be bad enough and ruin Liverpool and Bristol as well as many other towns. Many people had a vested interest in it, and Wilberforce was a shrewd politician and knew that you usually had to tackle one thing at a time if you were to get anywhere, even if you were going to be charged, as he was, with failure for not attacking other evils equally. This problem has a very modern ring. To ask for too much at once is often to jeopardise any smaller gains.

When after the passing of the Abolition Act, a deeply thankful group of friends had retired to Wilberforce's place in Palace Yard, he had asked: 'What shall we abolish next?'. Thornton suggested the lottery, but the answer that emerged was that they would tackle slavery itself,[12] though they did not realise then how much remained to be done on the Trade. Times had however moved on. The Quakers and others, who had been pioneers in the matter of rousing public opinion on the Trade by local meetings and then presenting petitions to Parliament, had not altogether forgotten the matter of liberation. By sustained use of all the media that were at their disposal the new campaign began to capture the public mind. Evangelical thinking was also spreading rapidly amongst the rising middle class of business people and other reasonably wealthy families. Some of this was due to the influence of Charles Simeon on numerous Anglican clergy; some was the filtering down of the results of the Methodist revival. Above all the Bible was being read and taken seriously in numerous homes. Family Prayers, that had been rare, were now very common and almost always involved the head of the house in reading and commenting briefly on a biblical passage. Even Ford K Brown, in his unsympathetic but well documented study of 'The Age of Wilberforce',[13] has to admit that this period saw a striking change in the general moral assumptions of society. He thinks it is largely due to the influence of the evangelical party in the Church of England; others think it was due to the influence of the second generation of those touched by the Methodist revival and still others point to the increasingly powerful influence of the Baptists and other Free Churches.

The fact is that there was a change towards a far greater awareness of the scandals of social evils and a desire to remedy them. The Slave Trade issue had formed a focus for a while. With the abolition of the Trade activity had to some extent subsided, but there was a massive fund of good will and even indignation about moral issues that the new programme could tap into so as to arouse public concern.

The African Institution became less active and was finally wound up in 1827. In the spring of 1823 however a new body *The Anti-Slavery Society*[14] had been set up with many of the same people on the committee. They had been stalwarts of the Slave Trade battles, including Wilberforce, Clarkson, Zachary Macaulay and William Allen (the Quaker Pharmacist, who was a life long anti-slavery activist). There were added some new and younger ones: Samuel Gurney (Hannah Buxton's younger brother) T.B. Macaulay and of course Buxton. The Duke of Gloucester was President of both societies. This was the society whose full title was interestingly: 'The Society for the Mitigation and Gradual Abolition of Slavery throughout the British Dominions'. There was a widespread belief that the slaves, who had usually had no opportunity of either education or religious instruction since they were plucked out of a tribal life in Africa, were simply not ready for full freedom. Hence the stress on 'gradually'. The slave masters also needed time to get used to the idea and to change their thinking, or so it was assumed by many. The planters were very nervous. The French possession of Saint Domingue (now Haiti) had seen a slave rebellion, with considerable bloodshed, followed by independence, when the ideas of the French Revolution had reached it, and the result had become chaotic. There had also been some slave rebellions particularly in

Jamaica, though they had been put down with great savagery, some rebels being burnt alive, progressively dismembered or shut in cages in public to starve to death. The planters were aware that almost everywhere they only held the whole regime together by violence and vicious punishments. To Buxton, however, it was becoming clearer that the whole system had to be destroyed as quickly as possible and that there were no real possibilities of doing it gradually. One must not deny the contribution that these brave rebels played in the long run to liberation, but they were not in the least likely to have succeeded against the massive vested interests in Britain unless the British government took decisive action to force it. That they were as yet unwilling to do, partly because their majority in both Houses often depended considerably on the 'West Indian' vote.

It has been argued, especially by some with a largely economic view of history, that the economics of the sugar islands had changed so much that slavery was perhaps no longer profitable and that this was the major factor in the success of the campaign. Professors Temperley and Anstey show that this is very unconvincing. Also if it had been true why did the West Indians and the Government

A convoy of slaves being taken by other Africans to the coast for sale to European traders.

resist liberation for so long? Why did other countries continue to import slaves on a very big scale and why did people with vested interests predict economic collapse if freedom was given? The USA, Brazil and Cuba certainly found slavery profitable for another thirty years and then did not give way for economic reasons. Temperley concludes a discussion of this claim by saying that 'the attack on it (slavery) must have been motivated by other considerations (than economic). On present evidence it would appear that these were primarily religious and humanitarian in origin'.[15]

The 'evangelical dynamic' of the anti-slavery movement, while not the sole impetus, was the essential element in its success. Its support in Britain was broadened by other factors, but it was neither initiated by those factors nor provided with the on-going impetus and perseverance to carry it through to success.

At the same time the idealists were calling for immediate liberation whatever the consequences. The aims of the new society were therefore seen by many idealists as far too cautious, though its opponents spoke of them as dangerously revolutionary and likely to lead to rebellion by the slaves and all sorts of further erosions of the established order. Clarkson did another extremely energetic tour of the country to reactivate the old anti-slavery committees and get them to send in more petitions. He quickly had 71 active groups and the number increased steadily to over 1000, with thousands of petitions to Parliament. A very powerful grassroots agitation was gaining ground.

CHAPTER 6

Parliamentary Battles, Chiefly on Slavery

MEANWHILE BUXTON AND Wilberforce had not been idle. Wilberforce's speaking had for some time been less effective. A while before this Buxton had said of his speeches: 'he takes no pains'. He had relied on his oratorical powers and now he began to ramble. Since his victory on the Trade however he had enormous prestige, both in Parliament and in the country as a whole. It was agreed by the leaders that it was Wilberforce who should write a pamphlet and, after struggling somewhat because of poor health, he published this in March 1823 under the title *An Appeal to the Religion, Justice and Humanity of the Inhabitants of the British Empire on Behalf of the Negro Slaves in the West Indies*. In the same month he opened the parliamentary campaign by presenting a petition for liberation from some Quakers. He was asked in reply whether he intended to base a motion on it and said: 'It was not, but that such was the intention of an esteemed friend of mine'.

Buxton then gave notice that on May 15th he would submit a motion. In the meantime he wrote to the government to explain the chief contents, inviting then to comment if they wished and stating that he was 'not absolutely determined' on the detail. He gave twelve proposals including that slaves 'cease to be chattels in the eyes of the law'; that their testimony in court be received as equal to anyone else's; that obstructions to manumission should be removed; that no governor or judge in these territories should be a slave-owner; that provision should be made for their religious instruction; that marriage be sanctioned and enforced and that limits should be set on punishments. Finally he proposed that the children of slaves be automatically free and given education. May 15th was the first real debate on the subject of liberation. On the day Buxton rose to propose 'That the state of slavery is repugnant to the principles of the British Constitution and of the Christian Religion; and that it ought to be gradually abolished throughout the British Colonies, with as much expedition as may be found consistent with due regard to the to the well-being of the parties concerned'. He was still using the word gradually.

George Canning, who was Leader of the Lower House in Lord Liverpool's government and also since 1821 Foreign Secretary, replied. He and Lord Liverpool clearly thought Buxton's motion far too radical and Canning , without warning Buxton, proposed amendments that took most of the force out of it. He agreed that something needed to be done, and that was a step forward, but he proposed only that they should 'adopt effectual and decisive measures for ameliorating the condition of the slave population'. He also insisted that it should be left to the colonial legislatures to implement some of Buxton's proposals and that these things should be done 'in a judicious and temperate' way and 'with a fair and equitable consideration of the interests of private property'. (One should note the emphasis on property, which is of course how slaves were regarded.) Wilberforce, who rose to reply, was caught by surprise by Canning's move and without opportunity of discussion with Buxton appeared to accept Canning's very watered down amendments, which were then passed. Buxton could not openly disagree with Wilberforce in the House and most of the more important of Buxton's proposals were set aside. Canning had not played fair with Buxton, who had consistently told him what he would propose.

This was of course very disappointing, but no one had thought that it would go through easily. The 'West Indians' in Parliament said that even the discussion of the matter in the House was dangerous, lest it stirred up unrest. Buxton followed this up with letters and a long interview with Canning on which he took careful notes and submitted them to Canning for agreement. He was always careful for detail, and since Canning seemed personally sympathetic, he wanted to know what exactly the Government would support. He had no intention of being caught out again by a government move to undermine apparently agreed proposals and nothing was likely to succeed if it was opposed by the Cabinet. If possible he wanted to get them to support liberation in the light of its growing popular support. Canning gave a verbal assurance that if the Colonies did not act the Government would compel them to do so – an assurance at least implied later in Parliament.

On May 28th Lord Bathurst (Colonial Secretary) wrote to the Colonial Governors, telling them of the situation and enclosing Canning's speech. A little later he wrote again urging them, but not compelling them, to adopt those measures that Parliament had agreed. These started with the provision of religious instruction and Christian education. The planters usually feared that this would render the slaves restless under the yoke. They often blamed the missionaries for making the slaves discontented, and of course there was something in this when they saw themselves as equal with their masters before God. The letter also urged that objections to manumission be removed, that slave families no longer be broken up (e.g. at auction), that the usually indecent flogging of women be discontinued, that punishments be generally moderated and that these matters be included in local law as soon as possible. The suggestion of freeing children and other proposals were ignored.

The planters were furious at this interference with their "rights" and almost universally ignored the proposals. Jamaica even talked of declaring independence of Britain and putting themselves under the protection of America. The 'Jamaica Journal' called the liberation party:

> those canting hypocritical rascals..... We will pray the Imperial Parliament to amend their origin, which is bribery; to cleanse their consciences, which are corrupt; to throw off their disguise, which is hypocrisy; to break with their false allies, who are the saints; and finally to banish from among them all the purchased rogues, who are three fourths of their number.[1]

Parliament was accused of having adopted 'the principles of the enemies of the colonies'. When the Order in Council reached Demerara (now part of Guiana) the authorities also talked of independence of England but tried to keep the Order secret, with exactly the opposite result. Rumours that they had already been set free and that the planters had suppressed the fact circulated quickly and on some estates the slaves refused to work and marched peacefully and unarmed demanding immediate liberation. A crowd of up to 13,000 was involved and the Governor, who was a slave owner, called out the militia and the few available troops, replying with violence. At least 100 slaves (no whites) were killed and brutal floggings were continued for some months with further death sentences under martial law. Three slaves were sentenced to the horrendous punishment of 1,000 lashes, which usually resulted in death. False reports appeared in the British Press that white men had been murdered.

A missionary of the London Missionary Society[2], John Smith, was imprisoned on a suspicion of having some responsibility, tried illegally and sentenced to death. Smith had never been strong physically, was mistreated and died in prison before he could be executed. This aroused great indignation in Britain, where he was spoken of as a martyr and his death and the brutal behaviour of the planters did much to lose the planters any sympathy in the general public view.

In Jamaica, the Assembly discovered, on the most dubious evidence, that there was a 'plot' and eight slaves were hanged.

In Barbados a mob of planters attacked the Methodist Chapel with dung and fireworks etc. When the authorities did not respond they planned and carried out an attack in which they demolished the Chapel and Manse, blaming the missionary, Mr Shrewsbury, for being in sympathy with government decisions. He had to flee for his life. The planters then called for the total elimination of Methodism from the island and urged other islands to do the same, claiming that evangelical faith was undermining the servility of the slaves. News of these and similar events stirred up the churches at home, particularly the Free Churches. Other reports of cruelties inflicted on the slaves by indignant planters were circulated by Clarkson to the local anti-slavery associations. Petitions began to pour in to Parliament. Nevertheless, from the point of view of the parliamentary programme, the news from the colonies could hardly have been worse. The predictions of unrest and bloodshed seemed to have begun to be fulfilled, though it was in fact the planters and not the slaves who were guilty. Wavering MPs left the cause. The Liberationists were widely blamed for all the troubles. Buxton, however, was unmoved and encouraged by Wilberforce, who knew what it was to be defeated at first, he never wavered. He was an obstinate man and also a brave man as various incidents showed. He had been nearly drowned going into the surf to rescue some men in a ferocious storm from a shipwreck near Cromer and in 1816 had risked his life to capture with his bare hands a mad dog that had already bitten several others. He now set to work to develop a new plan of attack. Angry with Canning's tactics he declared that he was going to 'go to war'.

On January 14th, 1824 he is writing to Zachary Macaulay:

> I have had the satisfaction of finding Wilberforce in good health. He seems by no means discouraged about our cause. Clarkson appears to have done his work well. At Norwich, our friends were somewhat intimidated; but he had a meeting there, which revived all their ardour... I have been hard at work, reading and making extracts from all the parliamentary slave papers.

There were no parliamentary secretaries or researchers then. Buxton developed a plan to get freedom for all children under seven, with compensation to the masters. This would of course gradually destroy slavery. He wrote to his wife on Feb. 9th:

> I am intensely busy. On Saturday we had a meeting, to which I read my plan. The more I think of it the more I like it. We meet again on Saturday: in the interim, an attack will probably be made on us, which I am to answer. I hold my head very high in the matter, and mean to be rather bold in my defence. I expect to see Canning tomorrow; he seems very cold to me. [A little later he is] so languid with over thought, and over work, that I hardly know how to write. On Saturday, we meet Canning at twelve o'clock, and Brougham, and all the leaders of our party, at the Duke of Gloucester's, at three o'clock. Then we shall decide on our course. I am not one bit discouraged, and heartily wish a discussion could be brought about, as I think it would change public opinion. How much, how very much happier I am in my Cromer retreat, than in the midst of all this bustle and turbulence. When you come, I shall be quieter, I hope. I am obliged to attend constantly at the House.

A month later however he writes: 'We have had a very unsatisfactory interview with Canning... The Government mean to forfeit their pledge, and do next to nothing'. They were evidently frightened by the unrest. Again:

> The degree, I will not call it, of opposition, but virulence, against me is quite surprising. I much question whether there is a more unpopular individual than myself in the House just at the moment.
>
> I shall not be able to go down to Cromer; my absence would further intimidate our few friends, who are sufficiently timid as it is....I keep up my spirits pretty well, but what with the mental fatigue I have undergone, and the disappointments we have experienced, I cannot feel very light-hearted.

A further interview with Canning showed that the government had decided to 'yield to the West Indian clamour, and do nothing, except in Trinidad where there is no Colonial Assembly. This timidity is very painful'. Buxton's plan for the liberation of children was rejected by the government, who made it plain that they thought the now small Liberation party was responsible for the troubles. In response to a speech to this effect by Canning, Buxton replied sharply, ending with:

> You ventured to agitate the question: a pledge was obtained; you were, therefore, to be considered the holder of that pledge, to which the hopes of half a million people were linked. And then, fearful of a little unpopularity, and confounded by the dazzling eloquence of the Right Honourable gentleman [i.e. Canning], you sat still, you held your peace, you were satisfied to see this pledge in favour of a whole archipelago, reduced to a single island. [Then after recording some of the horrible cruelty of the planters] What I have now said, I have said from a sense of public duty. I have no hostility to the planters. Compensation to the planters, emancipation of the children of the Negro – these are my desires.... to which, as long as I live, my most strenuous efforts shall be directed.

As an aside it is interesting to quote his 15 year old daughter's impressions on attending the May 15th, 1823 debate:

> We went to hear the slavery debate. It went off with the greatest interest. Mr Brougham did make such a speech. I

think altogether it was the most entertaining thing I ever heard. His grave dry way of saying the most ludicrous or bitter things is inexpressible and indescribable. His squint at the person he is speaking of, is one of the most comical things in the world....How he did cut up the West Indians. It was delightful to hear him. Papa spoke twice, the second time it was the most spirited reply to all that had been said on the other side of the question. Thus ended the most deeply interesting debate, at about half past one in the morning. I shall not attempt to say how much I enjoyed it, suffice to say that it was one of the greatest, if not the greatest, treat I ever had, and that I shall look back upon it with the greatest pleasure, interest, and I will add, pride.[3]

The government had effectively blocked further progress for the present, though there was plenty of room for agitation in the country and for ensuring that the evils of slavery were known to an ever wider constituency. The inner circle of Buxton's team worked out between them who should speak on each issue and in June 1st 1824 Brougham, in presenting one of the numerous petitions that were now coming into Parliament, proposed a motion on the Smith case. A memorable and well publicised debate followed. Brougham was an extremely able speaker. He and Denman had made great popular reputations, when they had successfully defended Queen Caroline in her 'trial' at a time when public sympathies were overwhelmingly with her and against the King. Brougham was, however, easily tempted into such scathing attacks on his opponents that he was not popular in Parliament. Buxton had studied his style and deliberately did not follow his example. Even Buxton's fifteen year old daughter could see the difference.

Brougham pointed out that it was because of the teaching of Smith that the slaves had agreed not to use violence or take life, but that they had been met with gratuitous slaughter. Smith had in fact saved the planters' lives not threatened them. Sir James Mackintosh, Dr Lushington and Wilberforce followed. It seems that Buxton did not speak. He had probably already retired for the summer to Cromer exhausted. There he rested and collected more information for future debates. Later that month Wilberforce renewed the issue and managed to extract a promise that the Canning resolutions would be enforced in St Lucia and Demerara, where also there was no Colonial Legislature to obstruct them. These were small gains, but the 350,000 slaves in Jamaica, 70,000 in Barbados and another probably 400,000 in the 15 other colonies continued to be treated almost as if nothing had been decided by London. In September Buxton, Lushington and Macaulay met every morning for some time after breakfast in Cromer to make plans.

The June debates were Wilberforce's last speeches in Parliament and early in 1825 he gave Buxton the honour of moving the writ for his retirement, in a speech that quoted part of the inscription on Hannibal's tomb. 'We vehemently desired him in the day of battle'. Wilberforce continued to speak at public meetings sometimes and to advise the leaders, but his health was uncertain and Buxton notes that he did not always keep to his theme. Buxton was left as unequivocally the leader of the cause.

These June debates, especially the Smith case, had caught the public attention and it is stated that public opinion began to move even more strongly in favour of liberation. Although the government was determined to do nothing more, a good deal of progress was possible through the circulation of literature, posters and public meetings organised by the local Auxiliaries.

The government began to realise that they could not entirely ignore the public, but at this point admitted that liberation was only likely if public opinion forced it on them. At the 1830 and 1832 elections all candidates were to be questioned by the local associations as to their stance on slavery and Christians were urged only to support those who gave a good answer. This was probably the first time such a moral issue had been used in that way. The Hull Association, for instance, published a list in the local press giving details of the attitudes of all candidates.[4]

In June 1825 Buxton provoked a debate on the treatment of the Methodist missionary in Barbados, Mr Shrewsbury. One of his crimes was said to be that he had corresponded with Buxton – a charge that Buxton could flatly deny: 'I never received from or wrote to him a single letter; nor did I know that such a man existed, till I happened to take up a newspaper, and there read, with some astonishment, that he was to be hanged for corresponding with me'. Shrewsbury had in fact taken refuge in the Anglican minister's vicarage and escaped the island to the credit, as Buxton said, of the

Anglicans, who were not famous for sympathy with the Free Churches in the Colonies and had often sided with the planters. The Free Churches at home were now aroused. As David Hempton put it: 'It was not until the 1820s that the anti-slavery movement enjoyed the mass support of an increasingly powerful Nonconformity'.[5] This also brought in many working class people, some of whom were by then influenced by a radical libertarian strand of politics and coupled freedom of the slaves with other freedoms. The support of Daniel O'Connell and other Irish nationalists, broadened the popular platform.

Although Canning was now more friendly and professed that he was going to do something, he would not say what it was. When in March 1826 Buxton presented a petition from 70,000 Londoners the debate led Canning to declare that the government intended 'to give the West Indians another year' before any legislation would be proposed by them and without their support a motion had no chance of success.

Shortly after that Denman (soon to become Lord Chief Justice) raised a debate on the injustices of the Jamaica trials, proposing a vote of censure on those responsible. The House would not agree, but these debates gave opportunities to present to the House and so, through reports in the Press, to the nation, some of the worst cruelties involved in slavery as it was practised in most areas. The exceptions were acknowledged, but they were very few. While waiting for the proposed further year to pass there was plenty to do to arouse opinion that could put pressure on the government and to collect more information. The planters always tried to present a rosy picture of slavery and incontrovertible evidence of the real situation needed to be presented constantly.

The Mauritius Slave Trade, Suttee and South African Blacks

During this quiet year for the West Indian slavery issue in Parliament (not in the country) Buxton received a visit from a Mr Bryam, who had been head of the police in Mauritius, and was indignant at the abuses he had seen and the fact that the Trade was continuing there on a large scale although it was no longer legal. Mauritius had been ceded to Britain from France only in 1810, but that was three years after the Trade was abolished in all British territories. Buxton set to work to confirm this report and to collect information with his usual meticulous care. On May 9th, 1826 he presented the case to Parliament, having collected the evidence from two of the three governors, four naval captains, five high civil servants and others. From the returns of the number of the black population he showed that either the slave trade had been going on or each woman had had one hundred and eighty children! He described the horrors of the packing of slaves in the ships and other features but could not get more than a select committee to enquire if the Trade really was continuing.

This was interrupted by a fresh General Election, which proved extremely stormy in Weymouth. The Tory supporters tried to prevent the Whig voters from voting by blocking the polling booths and Buxton was standing as a Whig. One Tory candidate was said to be spending £1,500 per day, with free food and drink in the public houses etc. Buxton refused to compete with favours and made it plain that his supporters would not get handouts of any kind. In the end he was top of the poll by a small margin and the other Whig candidate was defeated in favour of three Tories (It was a four MP constituency).

Back in Parliament he renewed work on the Mauritius Trade. A recent ex-Governor of Mauritius who was an MP complained in the House that the authorities had been charged with neglect of duty and challenged Buxton to produce proof. Typically this forced Buxton into another round of collecting and sifting information so as to present a totally compelling reply. What he found upset him deeply. He left his papers and strode up and down the lawn saying: 'Oh, it's too bad, it's too bad! I can't bear it.' He was over-wrought and became very unwell.

A day had been appointed for the debate and he worked very hard to get ready, but had to take time off for recovery. Finally he collapsed in health and on the appointed day he was in a coma, having apparently had a stroke. The family were sent for to attend what appeared to be his death bed, but he recovered, though needing some considerable time for recuperation. He used the time for quiet introspection and Bible study, finding special help in David's faith in his troubles as set out in the Psalms. We have to remember that in the absence of antibiotics, or indeed of any very effective medicines, serious illnesses often took a very long time for recovery and Buxton's doctor applied the standard remedy of bleeding him.

During this time he offended Charles Simeon, when they were both staying at Earlham, by going out shooting rather than going with Simeon to a meeting that Simeon had come to attend. As a peace offering he sent Simeon a present of game and received a delightful reply, assuring him that there was no ill feeling, but that Buxton might like to send another parcel of game for a big party he was holding soon! Buxton in fact received quite a bit of criticism from Quakers and others for his enthusiasm for shooting, but always maintained that it, with riding and walking, were his best recreations and that he needed to relax at times. He was also genuinely interested in the environment and played the leading part in successfully reintroducing the Capercaillie into Scotland. He admired the splendid bird and sent his gamekeeper to Norway to capture some and bring them back to Scotland as a present for a generous host there, where they flourished.[6]

He also spent time on the question of Suttee in India (the practice of burning alive those women who had been widowed). Clarkson had raised the issue in public and missionaries had brought this to Buxton's attention. As the slavery business was largely in suspension, this and other matters took his time. When he heard that later in 1827 Lord William Bentinck had been appointed Governor General of India, he immediately went up to London to discuss the question with him and was delighted to find him entirely supportive. He followed it up with correspondence and had the satisfaction of hearing that, very soon after arriving in India, Bentinck made the practice illegal.

He had been approached in 1822 by a Dr Philip of the London Missionary Society in Cape Colony, South Africa, about the 'grievous state of degradation in which the Hottentots were held by the (white) inhabitants of the colony, and especially by the Dutch'. Now he had time and was sufficiently recovered to take the matter up. The term Hottentots was used to describe the original peoples of the area, now usually known as the Khoi. They were in some ways in a worse situation than slaves, because they were no one's responsibility and were being treated as cattle after being robbed of their own large herds. They had no legal status and could be mercilessly exploited. Even the slaves of the whites despised them. Buxton was concerned for their education and their civil liberties but until 1828 had been unable to do much. When he then took time to collect the evidence of abuses he gave notice of a motion for a petition to the King on behalf of 'the natives of South Africa'. To his pleasure the Government agreed to accept his proposal, provided that he did not speak to it! This must have been to prevent his gaining too much moral authority and prestige in the House. The result was that almost without trouble the Hottentots were given legal freedom and civil rights, officially equal to whites. He wrote, perhaps too optimistically:

> we have recorded a resolution of the House of Commons, with regard to the Hottentots, which is their Magna Carta; and which will spread liberty, and, with liberty, a thousand other blessings over that great and growing territory. [To J.J. Gurney he added that it had]....given entire emancipation to the Hottentots. If this proves true I shall be excessively delighted, and shall never say again that I am sorry that I went into Parliament; not that I did much in the business, but I flatter myself that I did a little.

They could now own property and Buxton helped in the establishment of agricultural settlements on the Kat river, one of which was named Wilberforce and another Buxton. He also helped to establish schools and by 1839 there were 16 schools with 1,200 pupils and a dramatic decrease in drunkenness and plenty of good work being done on the land. In fact the new Governor of the Cape, General Bourke, who was a humane man, had moved in the same direction at the same time and Buxton felt that something important had been accomplished. He was delighted but of course could not foresee the future. It is interesting that Livingstone, soon after he arrived in South Africa in 1841, wrote of the remarkable success of the missionaries amongst the Hottentots. The Christian Hottentots he said were 'far superior in attainments to what he had expected' and their worship reminded him of the old Covenanters of his homeland.[7] This success was a very real encouragement to Buxton and he followed it up with continuing interest and involvement. He was becoming more confident of success on liberation.

Catholic Emancipation and Parliamentary Reform

The Government was preoccupied with the question of Catholic Emancipation and Buxton and his co-workers in Parliament became in favour of it, in Buxton's case only after careful study of the question. When he found that his constituents were strongly against he held his peace on the matter for a while. Finally however he felt that he must vote for it in the House, writing: 'I am going to secure my non-election next Parliament by voting for the Catholics tonight. I really must vote, the peace and safety of Ireland depend on our vote'. He knew that he would offend not only Anglicans but even more many of the Free Church evangelicals. His time in Dublin may have helped him here and he, perhaps unwisely, spoke out rather violently against the 'Protestant Ascendancy' as a misuse of power and a hindrance to peace and true religion. (see p106)

In 1827 Lord Liverpool resigned in ill health and died. Shortly afterwards Canning who took over as Prime Minister died also. These deaths each led to a period of political uncertainty, partly because the Tories were sharply divided over the question of Catholic Emancipation. Lord Goderich took over, with Huskinson as Colonial Secretary, but that administration lasted less that six months to be succeeded by the Duke of Wellington's more conservative part of the Tory Party, with Huskinson and then from May 1828 Sir George Murray at the Colonial Office. That administration was notable for the passing in May 1829 of the Catholic Relief Bill. This enabled Catholics to sit in both Houses of Parliament and made them eligible for all offices of state except three – Lord Lieutenant of Ireland, Lord Chancellor and Keeper of the Great Seal. Wellington admitted that he had given way on this only because of the popular clamour for it and the fear that to refuse it could even bring civil war. Buxton's position was known and this had an entirely unexpected result in that, on some of the crucial votes later on, he received the support of Irish members in the House apparently partly because of his earlier support for them, though people like Daniel O'Connell saw liberation of the slaves as linked in principle with all liberties and so with the liberation of Catholics. Buxton's decision however seems to have been entirely a matter of principle.

With the issue of Catholic Emancipation out of the way the coast seemed clearer, but the country and Parliament were now preoccupied with the Reform movement, with which Buxton sympathised. Nevertheless he was not going to be put off his primary concern by what he saw as a less urgent moral issue. He continued a programme of massive sifting of documents and reports from the Colonies and other sources on slavery. Here he was greatly helped by a group of relatives. His unmarried sister, Sarah Maria, and his wife's cousin, Anna Gurney, ('the Cottage Ladies') with his daughter Priscilla and Andrew Johnston, who found Buxton 'a delightful chief to work for – so stimulating, yet so indulgent, and so ready to pay with lavish liberalities every effort made, however trifling'. Andrew Johnston became MP for St Andrews and was to marry Priscilla in 1834 and carry her off to Scotland. Up to that date, however, she was very busy helping him, and her departure led Buxton to complain that Andrew had 'stolen my secretary'. She was an enormous help and amongst other things put his numerous papers in order to the benefit of future generations. Without the help of this small hard working group he would have been very limited in collecting the relevant facts and figures that he needed to prove his points.

Northrepps Hall, which was the Buxtons' home for the majority of their lives. This drawing was by his 16-year-old granddaughter Ellen (later Mrs Robert Barclay), while Hannah Buxton was still living there. The house and garden are little altered today.

When in 1828 he had to leave Cromer Hall, as the owner wanted it again, he settled at Northrepps Hall nearby and near to 'The Cottage'. He rented the Hall from Gurney relatives, but lived there permanently until his death.

Anna Gurney was an extremely able person, with a command of several languages, which she had learned partly to help the numerous shipwrecked sailors who ended up on the nearby coast. She was also the first person to translate *The Anglo-Saxon Chronicle* into English. She had devised an improvement of the Breeches Buoy to rescue sailors from ships on the rocks, trying it out on a tree in the garden to the consternation of her staff who had to climb the tree to come down it! Although confined to a wheelchair since a childhood attack of poliomyelitis she was a tireless worker and a close partnership developed between the Hall and the Cottage that was to prove invaluable, especially as Buxton got older and was often in only moderate health. The Cottage sorted research material and other papers, wrote letters and even provided drafts of speeches for him, which he used substantially. Banville comments with much appreciation on the two ladies, who were active in local philanthropy and set up a school in Overstrand, where there was none. It still continues as the excellent Belfry school, with the letters B and G (for Buxton and Gurney) in coloured flintstones over the front of the old building. Overstrand is near Northrepps and they all seem to have attended the Parish Church at Overstrand just opposite the school.

CHAPTER 7

The Final Battle on Slavery

BUXTON RETURNED TO London for the new session of Parliament in early 1828 with his health still casting doubt over how much he could do. Of the eight recommendations from Canning none had been adopted except in the small colony of Nevis. The Government however was determined to continue with a policy of persuasion rather than compulsion. Accordingly in 1828 Sir George Murray sent another circular letter to all the Colonies strongly urging them to act.

Once more this was totally ineffective. In March one of the 'West Indian' MPs (Wilmot Horton) brought forward a motion as an excuse for an attack on the liberation party. While Buxton had collected some material to answer him he had been too unwell to put it together and he attended the House quite unprepared, expecting others to reply. Horton's speech was however very clever and the others of Buxton's group of any comparable ability were not present. Stirred into action by a very bitter criticism of his party, Buxton rose to the occasion. After a stinging comment on the accusations made in the last speech he continued:

> The honourable member has indignantly censured my honourable friend for introducing the phrases 'rights of men and laws of God' and I do not wonder that he is somewhat provoked at these obnoxious expressions; for one cannot think of slavery without perceiving that it is a usurpation of the one and a violation of the other. The right honourable gentleman, the mover of this motion, tells us that no one can reconcile the promise that we have given for the extinction of slavery, with a promise which we have given for a

due consideration of the rights of the parties interested. We are reduced to the alternative, he tells us, of sacrificing the planter to the interests of the slave, or the slave to the interests of the planter. If we are in that predicament, and must decide for the one or the other, my judgement is unequivocally in favour of the slave; and it is a consideration of the 'rights of man and the laws of God' which leads me to that unequivocal decision....

I would give the Negro all that I could give him with security; I would do every possible thing to mitigate and sweeten his lot and to his children I would give unqualified emancipation. Having done this I would settle with the planters. I am a friend to compensation – but it is compensation on the broadest scale....Do you ask compensation for him who has wielded the whip? Then I ask compensation for him who has smarted under its lash! Do you ask compensation for loss of property, contingent and future? Then I ask compensation for unnumbered wrongs, the very least of which is the incapacity of possessing any property whatsoever.

A friend wrote to J.J. Gurney; 'The whole House was carried along by his earnestness, cheered him vehemently, and listened attentively. He was much congratulated on the success of his reply.' It is interesting to note how double edged the concept of rights was (and often still is today). The plantation owners used it to defend private property (slaves). Buxton replied in kind, but he and his allies used it very little. Their appeal was to the fact that slaves were equally human beings, created by God, of equal value to Him and worthy therefore of equal honours to anyone else.

Little more could be done in that session however. Brougham also had a period of illness and Lushington was too busy with other matters outside the House, though they were able to get agreement that the already free people of colour should have the same rights as their white fellow citizens and this was a significant advance in principle, even if it did not affect very many.

Buxton had a further interview with the Colonial Secretary about the Mauritius Slave Trade, but was told that the government would consider it and that in any case they believed that the Trade had stopped. They had sent out a commission of enquiry etc. In fact when that commission reported in 1829 it totally justified all that Buxton had said. The Trade was continuing on a very considerable scale. This answered the ex-governor who had denied it and forced the government to move, albeit slowly, and against great resistance from those on the island who were running it. Only in 1830 was the matter settled and it was agreed that all the slaves illegally imported should be freed, though the new Colonial Secretary (Lord Goderich) insisted that the onus of proving or disproving the title to possession of the slave was to lie with the slave, not with the master. This of course was difficult for many, though a good number of slaves managed to do it and were forthwith freed.

Meanwhile there had been sporadic involvement in the matter of the penal code and in 1830 he played an important part in a motion for the abolition of the death penalty for forgery by initiating a petition from more than 1000 bankers to this effect.[1] The House of Commons passed a resolution to end it and, although it was thrown out by the Lords, the matter was passed soon after. Buxton always maintained that the death penalty should not be applied to offences against property. Sir James Mackintosh and others kept up the pressure and Buxton helped whenever he could, so that it was not long before the total of capital offences was reduced to eight and, writing in 1849, his son Charles can say that 'practically no executions now take place in England or Wales, except for murder or attempts to murder'. It could never be said of Buxton that he did not care about issues at home. When Daniel O'Connell famously said of the Irish: 'Oh! I wish we were all blacks! If the Irish people were but black, we should have the member for Weymouth coming down as large as life, supported by all the "friends of humanity" in the back rows, to advocate their cause'; he was chiefly calling for their help, though incidentally paying a considerable tribute to their powers in Parliament. Buxton did support him and O'Connell supported Buxton, but Buxton had different priorities and could not do everything at once.

Buxton was also involved in the local troubles in North Norfolk. In 1830 there were riots in the countryside starting with Kent, where they were suppressed with considerable savagery, leaders being hanged or transported to Australia. Unemployment rose in Norfolk with the introduction of new threshing machines to replace hand threshing. Labourers burnt hay stacks and smashed the machines. Lord Suffield with Buxton and others tried to help. Suffield, who was a considerable landowner, had a plan to give each household a plot of land, since the land around cottages was being swallowed into big farms. Banville records how, when a rather ugly crowd began to approach Northrepps Hall, a farmer warned Buxton to go to meet them armed. He went out with his two sons hand in hand, took sticks from the men for the boys and said that now he was armed the boys could arrest them. The joke defused the situation and local farmers agreed not to use the new machines at least for a while and to raise wages. The ring leaders were however imprisoned by the magistrates for criminal damage and riot and nine were transported to Australia.[2]

Buxton's sixteen year old son, Harry, now became terminally ill with tuberculosis and died. Buxton was deeply upset. He had much enjoyment with his children and had helped the boy to enter into country interests and sports. Banville, the gamekeeper, was also very upset. Evidently the boy was liked by the people around. He was a sincere Christian and died with a clear faith, to his father's consolation. 'It is most painful' the father said to a friend as he watched the slow and inevitable decline: 'most painful, and yet most full of comfort. As painful as it can be, and as comfortable as it can be.' Writing to another friend he says:

> My poor boy is at the gates of death. Today we took the Sacrament together....As a little child leans upon his mother, so our dear Harry leans upon his Saviour....He knows the event which is coming, and is prepared to meet it with entire serenity. He is truly 'walking through the valley of death' and, as truly, 'he fears no evil.' Excuse me for saying so much on a subject which engrosses all our thoughts.

Then however the same letter goes on:

> Our slavery concerns go on well: the religious public has, at last, taken the field. The West Indians have done us good service. They have of late flogged slaves in Jamaica for praying, and imprisoned the missionaries, and they have given the nation to understand that preaching and praying are offences not to be tolerated in a slave colony....I have 100, perhaps 150 petitions waiting for me in London, but I do not leave home at present.

He was right that the public was now aroused about the slavery issue. Macaulay in the *Anti-Slavery Reporter*, a book by George Stephen, a son of the Trade Abolitionist James Stephen (Snr), and agitations by the Auxiliaries were bringing about a change in attitude. Temperley states that there were more petitions to Parliament on this subject than on any other in the century, including even parliamentary reform.

It was now seven years since Buxton had first raised the issue in the House. He had then stated that although the aim was 'the extinction of slavery' it was not possible to do it all at once. The slaves needed to be prepared for freedom. Now it was clear that a much more drastic approach was needed. He wrote: 'We did not know, as we now do, that all attempts at gradual abolition are utterly wild and visionary'. There was no serious hope of the slaves being raised in competence while they were still slaves and the planters opposed to education and Christian teaching. For the previous three years the government had tried to persuade the planters to virtually no effect. The movement for liberation was now much more powerful in the country. In May 1830 a crowded meeting was held in London with a very frail Wilberforce in the chair. Buxton proposed the first motion: 'that no proper or practicable means should be left unattempted for effecting at the earliest period the entire abolition of slavery throughout the British dominions.' A similar meeting in Edinburgh produced a petition for immediate emancipation with 22,000 signatures. Other powerful local Auxiliaries, notably in Birmingham and Glasgow, held large meetings and presented petitions; the Glasgow petition having 31,000 signatures.

The Agency Committee appointed five salaried lecturers to tour the country and speak at meetings, one of them being George Stephen. He later claimed that there were as many as 1200 local Agencies created by their efforts. The Agency Committee gradually became a largely independent body, although it operated from the same address for a while. When in 1832 it formally separated there began to be some differences of emphasis which occasionally surfaced in criticism of the older body for its conservatism in relying on Parliament. To the Agency Committee the slavery question was essentially a religious and moral issue and the slow pace of progress in Parliament showed that a more direct appeal to the people was needed. Slavery was a 'sin' and needed to be tackled as such. You do not abolish sins gradually. The frictions between the two bodies did not yet appear in public, but it was inevitable that Buxton now began to come under some criticism from his own side for the slow pace of progress. Both bodies were heavily dependent on the same sources of income, especially from the Quakers. The Anti-Slavery Society itself, including Buxton, had now abandoned 'gradualism' as inadequate and in any case unpractical so long as the slaves were being denied education and religious instruction. All the anti-slavery groups were demanding that the Government act decisively to give freedom and equal civil rights to the slaves. Buxton and the Anti-Slavery Society were concerned with the British Colonies, which the Government could hopefully bring into line. They could have far less influence elsewhere.

The Agency Committee wanted to widen the programme and to concentrate on a world-wide anti-slavery agitation. They hoped to influence Governments in other countries to stop their Trade and to persuade America, which had officially ended its Trade in 1807, to adopt liberation. They suggested that the abolition of the British Trade had done little more than change the flags under which it went on, since it was still continuing on a very big scale, particularly to Cuba and Brazil and in clandestine ways to North America and elsewhere. In fact they achieved little in these directions in the next two decades. They were also mainly pacifists and disagreed with the use of the British Navy to patrol the West Coast of Africa. The Agency Committee then became a separate body that with rapid changes of name was usually called the Universal Abolition Society (UAS).[3] When asked why it did not have on its committee the 'distinguished veterans of the Anti-Slavery cause' they replied sharply:

> The old Anti-Slavery Society was timid, inactive and destitute of a well defined anti-slavery principle. It was therefore a matter of extreme difficulty to stir up the country to energetic exertion or to simultaneous action.... For these reasons it could hardly be expected that the Agency Committee would embarrass their future operations by a renewal of their alliance. They preferred confining their number to those individuals, who though less well known to the public, had proved themselves to be the most useful Allies and the most constant to Anti-Slavery principles.

This was extremely unfair to people like Buxton and Lushington, who had carried the burden of the day in Parliament and knew how to work there, but was not untypical of the sort of criticism that Buxton had to face from the more idealistic popular activists. Fortunately Buxton was not tempted into replies in public when attacked in this sort of way. He held his peace and, though he was constantly self-critical, held to his course, using the opportunities that he had to carry the cause forward. Such genuine misunderstandings of politicians have always been common, though it does no harm to them to hear such remarks and be made to justify their policies to themselves at least.

The Agency Committee sent one of their lecturers, George Thompson, to America, hoping for a good reception there and that he could further the liberation cause in USA. Lord Suffield had warned them that an English lecturer was not likely to get a good reception so soon after the War of Independence and proved quite correct. Thompson met with considerable opposition and achieved practically nothing. The Agency Committee in fact was able to gain little ground and was soon wound up, to be replaced by other societies with a bewildering variety of similar names.

The Reform Bills

In 1830 after 47 years of Tory domination, which had included only short periods of coalition, a Whig government was elected under Earl Grey as Prime Minister (in the House of Lords) and with Lord Althorp (another son of a Peer) as leader in the House of Commons. Reform had been in the air for a good long time and social unrest was common. The new government set to work quickly to carry out reforms and to put together the Reform Bills that would have wide ranging effects on the nature of Parliament and bring many more people onto the lists of voters by 1832.

Wilberforce, Buxton, and most probably all of their circle, were in favour of the reforms, though at the same time they were very anxious not to be associated with the radicals. They were strongly of the view that firm government was needed and that there was a danger of undermining the whole structure of society and so leading to the chaos of the French Revolution. It is easy to misunderstand their position and to present them as opponents of progress, which is not true. 1830 was also the year of the overthrow of the restored Bourbon monarchy in France, which was specially alarming to those in England who feared revolution.

Buxton amongst other things also believed in Free Trade and his attitude is partly illustrated by what he wrote on the Beer Bill, which adversely affected his own interests. This Bill removed a partial monopoly held by the twelve largest breweries, of which his was one. It looked like being a serious blow to his firm, though that was not immediately certain. He wrote to J.J. Gurney that he did not object to the change for:

> I have always voted for free trade, when the interests of others were concerned, and it would be awkward to change when my own are in jeopardy. Secondly, I believe in the principles of free trade, and expect that they will do us good in the long run, though the immediate loss may be great. And, lastly, I am pleased to have an opportunity of proving, that our real monopoly is one of skill and capital.

When he referred some years later to the enormous losses that this Beer Bill had brought to the British firms like his own he could remark: 'But it was right; it broke in upon a rotten part of our system – I am glad that they amputated us.' He was certainly trying hard to be consistent and not to be ruled in business any more than in Parliament by personal interest.

The years 1830-32 were a good deal dominated by the movement for the reform of Parliament. The return of Grey's administration had raised hopes of rapid progress both in parliamentary reform and in the slavery question. Brougham was now Lord Chancellor and, although he had hoped to further the liberation cause, he seems to have found his hands tied by other duties. The Associations had however been urged to question all parliamentary candidates as to their views on liberation and vote only for those who gave a good answer. By the 1832 election this had unseated some established MPs, replacing them with people more sympathetic to the cause. There were also still influential people at the Colonial Office, including James Stephen (Jnr) and Lord Glenelg, a son of Charles Grant who had been prominent in the Anti-Slave Trade cause, and his successor in office, Lord Normanton, who was equally helpful. The office holders changed rapidly, which hindered progress, but it became clear that, for whatever reasons, the Government was now firmly committed to liberation – before too long!

The Government, however, was preoccupied with the Reform Acts and social unrest had made the matter urgent. Banville comments that he wishes that as much attention was paid to the needs of the poor at home as to the needs of slaves in the West Indies, and presumably he has Buxton in mind here as well as others.

The first Reform Bill was introduced in March 1831, but was defeated. When it was introduced again in June it passed the Commons, after a series of Tory delaying amendments and several all night sessions, but was thrown out by the Lords. There were Reform riots all over the country, especially in Nottingham and Derby and notably in Bristol, where the Town Hall and other buildings were burnt down. Wilberforce is recorded as seeing the Bristol fires while trying to recover his health at Bath and being very concerned. Buxton attended the debates regularly and voted for the reforms but played no active part in the issue. It was not until June 1832 that the Reform Bill was passed and then only when the Lords were threatened with being flooded with new Peers who would support it and the Tory Peers therefore abstained. In December 1832 a new Parliament was elected under the new wider franchise and redistribution of seats, bringing in many more MPs (perhaps now 200 in total) sympathetic to the liberation cause. That however is to jump ahead.

Meanwhile in 1831 Althorp proposed some minor changes in slavery legislation on behalf of the Government. The repeated slavery debates in 1831 and 1832 included many references to the fact, which Buxton stressed, that the slave population was actually declining quite substantially. This was astonishing and could only be attributed to the fact that the slaves were being worked or mistreated to death. It did not apply where they had been freed. It was agreed that the small number of slaves belonging to the Crown should be freed. Like other half measures the result was most unfortunate. The slaves in Jamaica believed once more that the King of England had given freedom to all slaves. They went on strike because they had not been freed and started destroying some of the plantations. As before, this was without killing any whites, but was met by savage punishments. Seventeen chapels were destroyed by the planters and the missionaries were very badly treated.

Providentially two of the most impressive missionaries were expelled from the island and came home just in time to travel around Britain giving first hand accounts of the real character of slavery, including reporting to parliamentary committees. Most of the plantations were managed by agents, who had no interest except to extract the maximum financial return, and some of the 'West Indians' in Parliament perhaps did not really know just how cruel the system was. The anti-slavery lobby made maximum use of the facts, which Buxton was always careful to present in Parliament from official reports of punishments etc. rather than the reports of those who had suffered. He found plenty of incriminating facts in sources that the opposition could not disown. Because the plantation owners were generally absentees, the system in the British Colonies was frequently even worse than that in North America, where the owners were often resident and kept some sort of selfish humanity in regard to the way slaves were treated, so long as they could continue to regard slaves as their property, to be bought, sold or misused at pleasure.

The Government again took fright, fearing that liberation would lead to total disorder. They even voted money to restore the Jamaica plantations, as if Parliament had been to blame, and set up a committee of the Lords to consider the interests of the West Indian trade. The fear was expressed that, if freed, the slaves would all refuse to work and the whole economy collapse. The Government still argued that liberation should be postponed until 'a progressive improvement should have been made in the slave population, by a temperate enforcement of ameliorating measures'. Althorp threatened to propose an amendment in those terms if Buxton should persist in proposing a motion for immediate freedom as he was suggesting.

Sir Robert Peel 'shuddered to contemplate' the calamities that he believed would follow from rapid emancipation. It was widely maintained that the slaves needed considerable preparation for freedom, in view of the conditions in which they were held, and that there should be a long period of preparation. Indeed many opponents of liberation believed, or at least maintained, that the slaves were inherently incapable of using freedom aright however much they were prepared for it. They had never seen an educated African or one holding a responsible position and believed that they were constitutionally inferior to whites.

In May 1832, as the Reform Bill debates were coming to a conclusion, Buxton decided to force the issue. He announced that he would propose a motion for total liberation. MPs at that time could bring a motion before the House without a ballot or other complex preliminaries. He said that he would divide the House on the issue. The Government would not agree but realised that the degree of support he commanded might defeat them and bring them down and so jeopardise the whole reform process. It was a tense and very difficult decision. The Cabinet repeatedly begged him to withdraw or dilute his motion. Friends, even Lushington and Brougham, thought him foolish and for a few days hardly anyone in the House would speak to him, other than to express their disapproval. His friends in the Whig party appeared to be alienated. On the day of the debate he wavered, only to decide that 'the real interests of 800,000 slaves' compelled him go ahead. His daughter, Priscilla, described the day in a letter to the 'Cottage Ladies':

> Father and I went out on horseback directly after breakfast, and a memorable ride we had. He began by saying that he had stood so far, but that divide (the House) he could not. He said I could not conceive the pain of it, that numberless ties and interests were concerned, that friends would be driven to vote against him, and thus their seats would be endangered. But then his mind turned to the sufferings of the missionaries and the slaves. In short, by degrees, his mind was made up.... When we got near the House every minute we met somebody or other, who just hastily rode up to us. 'Come on tonight?' (i.e. will you press a division?) 'Yes'. 'Positively?'. 'Positively', and with a blank countenance, the inquirer turned his horse's head, and rode away....We came home and dined at three.

She then went with him to the House.

> Many Anti-slavery petitions were presented....At length, about six, 'Mr Fowell Buxton' was called; he presented two petitions....The order of the day was then called, and he moved his resolution, which was for a Committee 'to consider and report upon the best means of abolishing the state of slavery throughout the British dominions, with a due regard to the safety of all parties concerned.' He spoke very well indeed, and they listened to him far better than last year.

T.B. Macaulay and Lord Howick (a son of Earl Grey, the Prime Minister) supported him. Lord Althorp proposed a diluting amendment.

> Then came the trial; they (privately) besought my father not to press them to a division....He told us that he thought he had had a hundred applications of this kind, in the course of the evening; in short nearly every friend he had in the House came to him, and by all considerations of reason and friendship, besought him to give way....At length he rose to reply, and very touchingly alluded to the effort he had to make, but said, he was bound in conscience to do it, and that he would divide the House. The vote was taken and Lord Althorp's amendment was passed by 136 to 90....Mr ----- would not speak to him after it was over, so angry was he; and for days after when my father came home, he used to mention, with real pain, somebody or other who would not return his bow.

It was the sort of unpopular decision that he, more than most people, was willing to take. In retrospect it seems that he was almost certainly right to force the issue, though many friends disagreed. It proved to the government that in other circumstances liberation would command a substantial majority and that if they did not support it they might fall on the issue. Therefore they had better prove themselves positive. A few days after the debate, Althorp said to T.B. Macaulay:

> That division of Buxton's has settled the slavery question. If he can get ninety to vote with him when he is wrong, and most of those really interested in the subject vote against him, he can command a majority when he is right.

The Final Crunch

Buxton believed, rightly, that 'the cause made a seven-league stride' as a result of this debate. It had persuaded the Government that they would have to settle the question soon, by making it their own proposal, or risk losing all popular support and being defeated in the House of Commons. They had probably noted that at the 1832 election Buxton had been re-elected for Weymouth with the greatest enthusiasm and a large majority.

Nevertheless not everyone was pleased. On the eve of the election he had published a letter in which electors all over the country were urged to get pledges from the candidates that they would aim to bring in legislation in the terms of his own motion. Some of the idealists were angry that he had included a qualification to emancipation in terms of the phrase 'compatible with the safety of all classes'. One correspondent, and he was evidently far from unique, wrote:

> To be candid, Sir, I would rather see you throw up your brief, and take a retaining fee from the planters, than that you should, in a reformed Parliament, bring forward a motion in accordance with the sentiments expressed in that letter. And if you appear as an advocate of such a profane measure, we will look to some more enlightened advocate to forward that cause which must be carried.

Buxton replied generously:

> Dear Sir,
> I am so thoroughly inured to expression of the strongest condemnation from all sides, as to my course with regard to slavery, that I should scarcely be prevailed upon to notice those I have received from you, were it not that I like the spirit which dictates them, and should be glad if it were more general. With every good wish, and begging you to continue your exertions, and to blame me as much as you please, if it will stir up one of your friends, I am, dear Sir,
> Yours very truly,
> T. Fowell Buxton.

George Stephen, writing later about these battles and the pressure from right and left, says in a letter to Mrs Harriet Beecher Stowe: 'I verily believe that Mr Buxton was the only man in England who could have withstood it all'.[4] Seeing the end in sight Buxton was busy consulting with Lushington and the others. To Zachary Macaulay he wrote in December 1832:

> We must stick fast and firm to our claims for justice. Immediate and total emancipation is our right, and if we yield an iota of it, it must be, not for the sake of the planter, nor for the sake of the Government, but for the benefit of the Negro; and we must give up no more than it is in the interests of the Negro to surrender.

The House of Commons, 5th February 1833, the day on which the new MPs first met following the election under the reformed franchise. Buxton is seen side face standing in the middle of the front row on the left.

That of course left the question to be answered as to what would really be in the interests of the slaves. He was quickly involved with the Government in discussions of the way forward and found them now much more co-operative.

To the dismay of the liberation party, however, the King's speech at the opening of Parliament on Feb. 15th, 1833 contained no mention of business on the slavery question. Buxton immediately gave notice of a motion and this triggered Lord Grey into action. The Government gave an assurance that they would introduce legislation for 'a safe and satisfactory measure' and this persuaded Buxton to withdraw his motion. MPs were left in no doubt by their constituents that, now that the Reform issue was settled, the slavery issue was the number one public concern. His daughter again writes to the Cottage Ladies: 'So it appears that there is quite a band in the House and an army out of it. My father is very often with the ministers, and seems on the whole well satisfied.' He was willing to give the leadership of the matter to the ministers, so long as he could keep a careful check on what they were doing. This raised the suspicion amongst some of his supporters outside Parliament that he was currying favour with the Government and he was accused by them of being too anxious to please – an accusation that hurt him because he was always very self-critical as to his motives. He was, however, sure that there would be no satisfactory conclusion unless the Government itself took the lead and confronted the vested interests in and out of Parliament. Friends commented that he seemed not to care in the least whether he got any credit for emancipation as long as it was done in the best way. The Government were keen to get any credit and that suited Buxton so long as it got the matter settled in a good way. Lord Howick, who was friendly, was now Under-Secretary at the Colonial Office. Buxton had agreed to give up his motion in view of the promised Government measure, but nothing seemed to be happening and he became anxious and almost depressed. Rumours circulated that the Cabinet were divided and might compromise again.

The date that he had originally proposed for the motion that he then withdrew was March 19th. When by the 16th nothing had happened he announced that he would after all propose his motion. The Government then arranged parliamentary business to deprive him of the opportunity. On 18th he went to the House, sat behind Althorp, and argued with him. In the end Althorp said: 'Well if you will not yield we must', and agreed to fix a date for a measure including their proposals. They again tried to stall, but Buxton was so incensed that he crossed the floor of the House to speak from the opposition side! He had to be extremely tough, and few others would have been able to do it. He stated that unless the Government would firstly propose a plan for the complete abolition of slavery and fix a date for a measure to that effect he would propose his motion. Althorp then named April 23rd for his Cabinet motion and Buxton accepted it. He knew that unless a date was given in that session of Parliament it would almost certainly be lost for a long time. Delay was very dangerous also, because the slaves were informed about what was going on and there was a real fear of insurrection on a huge scale, with bloody responses from the planters, if the matter was postponed. At one point Buxton had written in a private memorandum: 'How should I feel if there was an insurrection and 50,000 perished?' Opponents made out that that was a serious possibility and had blamed him for even raising the question of liberation in Parliament.

Buxton now saw the end in sight and relaxed a bit. He slept better and recovered in health, though it was not clear what exactly would be in the Government's plans. The need for continual public pressure was clear to all the liberation party. A special committee of the Anti-Slavery Society was called and there were further meetings with Lushington and others. Just then a man named Whiteley returned from the West Indies with the usual stories of cruelty – the chained gangs taken out to the plantations, the break up of families, the thrashing of stripped women, tied down while the cart-whip cut into their flesh, and that without trial and on mere hearsay evidence, or on the whim of the planter, etc. Buxton realised that this could help and got him to write it up. Its simple but telling graphic details caught the popular imagination. Within a few weeks 200,000 copies had been circulated. His daughter wrote: 'the sensation it creates is immense: the printers can scarcely supply the demand.' The popular demand for liberation grew in intensity with meetings all over the country to provide petitions to Parliament. While agitating in the country, however, they were anxious to keep friendly co-operation with the Cabinet as far as was possible. It was agreed amongst supporters to plan a nation-wide day of prayer, Buxton writing a letter to Anglicans to urge them to join in this with the Free Churches who were prominent.

It emerged that the first concession wanted by the Cabinet was that there should be compensation to the planters. Buxton and his close allies agreed. It cost the slaves nothing and it seemed to be the best way to ensure that there was a peaceful transition, so that the planters would have no excuse for a burst of savagery before emancipation took place. It also made it much more difficult for the 'West Indians' in both Houses of Parliament to oppose the legislation.

The Annual Meeting of the Anti-Slavery Society was due in April. Buxton had to try to justify this and other concessions. With Lord Suffield in the chair, Buxton, Lushington and J.J. Gurney spoke, apparently with acceptance even to the Agency leaders. The latter needed the MPs and co-operation was maintained, even though there was some growing criticism from the Agencies of the acceptance of compensation. A formidable gathering of Agency representatives was called in London and some of them marched in a body to Downing Street, where Buxton introduced delegates from all over the British Isles to the new Colonial Secretary, Stanley, who had succeeded Lord Goderich when the latter became the Earl of Ripon and Lord Privy Seal. This included representatives from Ireland (Cork and Belfast), Wales (Carmarthen), several from Scotland and all over England. It was impressive and must have made some impact on the Government. The delegates retired for a meal and Buxton took the opportunity of paying a tribute to the ageing Macaulay, calling him 'the real leader of this cause – the Anti-Slavery tutor of us all'. The battle was not over, but Althorp said to Lord Suffield a little later: 'Lushington and Buxton have wielded a power too great for any individuals in the House. I hope we shall never see another such instance'. The repeated challenges to the Government's inactivity seemed at last to be having their effect.

Things, in fact, now moved with unusual speed. Everyone waited for the Government's measure, which had by agreement been postponed to May 14th to allow time for the details to be worked out. Proceedings began with Buxton presenting a petition from the women of Britain, who of course had no vote. It had 187,000 signatures on a series of sheets from different parts of the country and was so heavy that Buxton had to ask for the help of three strong members of the House to carry it in, to the laughter and cheers of the House. Stanley opened the debate covering some of the facts of the situation that the abolitionists had often stated. The death rate of the slaves due to ill treatment was so high that the slave population was declining. As the number of slaves declined, so the number of punishments increased to try to get the same work out of fewer workers. The government was constantly disappointed that the Colonial Legislatures had failed to act on advice etc.

It was good to hear these things repeated by the Government. He then turned to the practicalities. The first was that the slaves should be legally free citizens, but that they would be bound to work for the planters as apprentices for three quarters of the day in return for food and clothing, leaving them one quarter to cultivate their own plots. This was to last for eleven years. All children under six were to be unconditionally freed and paid 'supervisors' were to be appointed from London to control the apprenticeship scheme. Positive steps were also to be taken for the religious instruction and education of the apprentices and their children. Apprentices were, however, still to be subject to physical punishments if they did not give their share of their time to the work. A loan of £15,000,000 would be made to the planters to tide them over the transition.

This was not all that the Liberation Party had hoped for, but it was a huge advance and it recognised the principle that slaves must be freed. Now at last they were forcing it on the Colonies. It was hoped that some of the concessions could be changed at the Committee stage of the Bill, but they dared not oppose it at either first or second reading and so risk the whole. That would almost certainly have created bloodshed in the islands. The parliamentary group agreed to accept the measure in principle and resorted to prayer about the final form of the Act and the response there might be in the Colonies.

At the Committee stage, preparing the final form of the Act, they were in fact able to make some important improvements. Buxton proposed a reduction of the period of apprenticeship to one year and was only defeated by seven votes. This led Stanley next day to offer to reduce it to seven years, and later to six on the plantations and four for domestics. As a compensation, however, the loan of £15,000,000 was changed to an outright gift of £20,000,000 to be distributed in proportion to the planters. Buxton was also defeated on many of his other proposed amendments, but the freeing of all children under six was maintained. The 'generosity' of the compensation to the planters was a surprise to most people, but the Cabinet were caught between the pressure of the Liberation Party and the powerful 'West Indians' in both Houses, who pleaded imminent poverty. They also wanted to get it all settled. Buxton's group in Parliament accepted it as the best that they could get, particularly as the compensation cost the slaves nothing.

Outside Parliament it was another matter. Buxton was bitterly attacked in the Agencies, and in some of the Press, for accepting concessions, particularly the financial compensation, which was seen as paying people for evil done. His daughter again writes of:

> many personal humiliations and mortifications; and now the Anti-Slavery people are so violently turned against my father for not voting against the twenty millions, that they

can hardly find words to express their displeasure. I must say that his spirit through all is wonderful....Every day he receives violent letters of censure.

On July 1st the Bill was presented to Parliament in its revised form, and on August 7th the Act for 'The Total Abolition of Colonial Slavery' passed the House of Commons. On 20th it passed the House of Lords, after Lord Suffield had argued it through clause by clause. On August 28th it received the Royal Assent. All slaves were to be free people on August 1st 1834. Buxton immediately wrote off to Clarkson, with a copy of the Act, saying how much it owed to the latter's efforts over the years. There was much satisfaction and rejoicing, in which some of his supporters outside Parliament could not join wholeheartedly, as they regarded it as a blameworthy compromise. Buxton's reputation with these people never recovered totally.

Wilberforce died while the Act was going through its second reading, living just long enough to hear that the crucial points had been agreed and that the Act seemed to be secure. He was buried with great ceremony in Westminster Abbey, his reputation unsullied. What he would have done in Buxton's situation is unknown, but he was a shrewd politician and one can guess that he too would have agreed the concessions made by Buxton as necessary to getting it through.

The Aftermath

There were serious apprehensions as to how the Act would be received when it reached the Colonies. When news returned it was most encouraging. The Colonial Legislatures accepted it and began taking steps to put it into effect. The planters seemed to be satisfied with the compensation and the slaves had also accepted it without either the feared over-reaction or with deep disappointment that liberation was not total and immediate. Even Buxton expressed himself as surprised at how well his prayers had been answered. One of the group commented to Buxton: 'This is worth living for and dying for'. He relaxed for a while with his family at Northrepps helping his children to enjoy the country, especially swimming in the cold sea at Cromer! He wrote that he had ridden 500 miles and walked 1500 in that year.

When amongst others Stanley congratulated him, Buxton replied: 'I congratulate you', and when Stanley reported the good news from the Colonies to Parliament all the liberation party were delighted and in a remarkable turn-around they were greeted with great warmth by MPs of all parties. He became busy with the work of the 'Supervisors' and the provision of the agreed religious and educational programme. The Bible Society promised to give a New Testament and Psalter to every Negro who was found able to read on the Christmas Day after emancipation. A Trust Fund, whose original aims for slaves could not be fulfilled, was legally allowed to be used for the education programme, with Buxton and Lushington now amongst its Trustees. It moved fast and the Government even gave a further £20,000 towards it. They set to work to train teachers for the new schools and, working with the missionary agencies of all denominations, they trained 500 teachers before very long. Buxton tried to meet each batch of teachers before they left, shake each by the hand and wish them well. Primary school teachers in those days were mostly of humble origin and on one of these occasions Buxton had to hurry from the Royal Court without time to change. His appearance in full court dress astonished the teachers, and the personal warmth of his greeting in spite of it made a deep impression. He made them realise that he really cared for them and their work.

As August 1st 1834 approached there was still nevertheless a good deal of anxiety as to what would happen. For so long dire predictions had been circulated of bloodshed, rioting, drunkenness and general disorder. The Governor of Jamaica had arranged for troops and naval vessels to be available to quell any disorders. It was not until 10th Sept. that news arrived. Five weeks was an average time for crossing the Atlantic. Buxton received a packet of letters with colonial stamps at Northrepps and carried them off unopened into the woods to read them on his own.

The news could hardly have been better. There were virtually no unpleasant incidents and none of them were serious. No one was hurt, no property was destroyed and almost everywhere the slaves had packed the churches and chapels as midnight on the day approached. As the hour struck they burst into songs of praise and thanksgiving. August 1st had fallen on a Friday and the week-end had been one of entirely peaceful jubilation. On the Monday they were back at work as usual, contrary to predictions that they would just refuse to work in their new status. It was a truly remarkable triumph and Buxton and the others were profoundly thankful to

God. Thanksgiving celebrations were held in many parts of Britain. Buxton's daughter, Priscilla, had chosen Liberation Day for her wedding to Andrew Johnston at Northrepps, so there were double celebrations there, starting with a presentation to Buxton of inscribed silver plate from his nephews and nieces to mark Liberation Day (which moved him to tears), then the wedding and huge parties in the villages, with over 300 children and speeches about the liberation.[5]

It is popular today to point out that the plantations were not as profitable as they had been, that the slave rebellions of the previous years had contributed much to the change and that other social factors helped. There is probably some truth in all these points, but the fact is that this was an entirely peaceful transition and that it was carried in the country by a massive moral campaign in the face of powerful economic interests. It had, for instance, been stated in a letter to *The Times* that liberation would mean that 'The lives and property of millions of our fellow subjects must necessarily be subjected not only to risk, but for the greatest part to inevitable destruction.'[6] Clearly the planters believed that slavery was very profitable. The Government, however, could not resist the combined public and parliamentary pressure. The campaign only succeeded when it did, and not very much later and probably with much bloodshed, through the most tenacious group of strongly Christian MPs, who had had to fight all the way for twelve years and more against violent criticism from all sides. They had depended on Clarkson, Macaulay and a whole national campaign outside Parliament. It was in many ways an exemplary campaign of Christian political action both in the country at large and in Parliament.

Buxton was not someone to sit back and wait for this news and, between the passing of the Act and the day of Liberation, he put time into the abuses of the indigenous peoples in the Colonies, particularly in South Africa. He was shocked by reports of the blatant greed and gross cruelty with which the whites had annexed tribal lands, stolen the cattle and killed great numbers of the 'Caffres' (= Kafirs, the Bantu peoples) on the least excuse, which was often something deliberately provoked. A despatch to Lord Glenelg from South Africa announced, apparently with great satisfaction that:

> 4000 Caffre warriors have been slaughtered: 60,000 head of cattle, and almost all their goats captured: their country

(now called Adelaide territory) is taken from them: their habitations are everywhere destroyed, and their gardens and corn fields laid waste.[7]

This sounds exactly like what we would now call ethnic cleansing. Buxton was outraged and was in frequent touch with the Colonial Office, where he found a much more sympathetic ear than before. He moved successfully in the House for a parliamentary committee to look into the matter and the general treatment of the aboriginal nations bordering on British lands. Soon he and his team at Northrepps were very busy on these questions. He writes to Zachary Macaulay:

> Oh we Englishmen are, by our own account, fine fellows at home. Who among us doubts that we surpass the world in religion, justice, refinement, and practical honesty? But such a set of miscreants and wolves as we prove when we escape from the range of the laws, the earth does not contain.

The Colonial Office under Lord Glenelg was quickly persuaded to take action to correct things and give compensation to those who had been wronged. South Africa was a long way away and there was much less information coming in and few vested interests in Parliament. Soon the Adelaide country was returned to the 'Caffres'. Buxton rejoiced and wrote to the Cottage:

> I have to tell you a piece of news, which has made me sing ever since I heard it... It is life itself, and liberty, and lands and tenements to a whole nation. It is nothing short of this; the hand of the proud oppressor in Africa has been, under Providence, arrested, and a whole nation, doomed to ruin, exile and death, has been delivered and restored to its rights. On a given day the drum was beat and the troops were marched directly back again to the British territory, and the fertile and beautiful Adelaide was once more Caffreland. Only think how delighted must our savage friends be, and with what feelings must they have viewed our retreating army! Surely we must make a party... This is, indeed, a noble victory of right over might.

Time was to show that these measures were not as effective in the long term as he hoped. He continued on the Parliamentary Committee on the aborigines questions and gave a lot of time to it.

He was also able to give more time than he had done for a while to the question of the Slave Trade that was still being carried on on a big scale by other nations. He was by no means the leader here, because the Agency Committee (which had been replaced by the Universal Abolition Society, known as the UAS), had made it their main concern. There was now a serious breach between the UAS, in which Sturge was a leader, and the parent body, in which the MPs were still the leaders. Buxton's main interest now became the implementation of the Act and the working of the apprenticeship scheme.

Apprenticeship

Antigua and Bermuda had taken the step of giving total and unconditional freedom immediately and this had been an unqualified success. The apprenticeship scheme, however, was in operation elsewhere and was still in the hands of the Colonial Legislatures, but in co-operation with the supervisors appointed from London. In a number of Colonies it did not work well, occasionally very badly. There were sometimes not enough supervisors and some of them sided more with the planters than the slaves. In Jamaica especially it worked badly owing to the attitude of the planters, and apprentices were no better off than they had been as slaves and in some ways worse off. The planters took advantage of the situation to deprive the ex-slaves of some of the things that had been taken for granted before, such as water carried to the work stations. Cruel punishments continued and there were even still chained gangs taken out to the plantations in some places. Some new punishments were introduced, including treadmills, which were so badly constructed that they inflicted terrible injuries. By April 1835 reports were causing considerable concern. It was clear that while the slaves had almost without exception behaved well the planters often had not. It was agreed that Buxton should raise the matter in Parliament and in June he moved for a Select Committee to look into it. The Government assured everyone that the abuses were only local and that they had these matters in hand, whereupon Buxton withdrew his motion. He had his reasons for this in his strategy about how best to harry the Government, but he failed to explain his reasons and again he came under severe criticisms from some of the other leaders outside Parliament. One wonders whether he had become a little too confident that he alone could handle the matter.

He and Suffield were attacked in public by the UAS. It appears that Buxton feared that some Colonies would try to reintroduce slavery and that he should hold his fire in case that happened. He says that he had only accepted apprenticeship at all in exchange for a clause, included in the Act, that when it ended freedom was to be absolute. That however could not prevent the Government from going back on this provision. When he was also found to have been involved in the arrangements for the compensation to the slave owners in Mauritius he was accused of having accepted the principle of compensation as a right. In fact he had never accepted it as other than politically expedient if liberation was to be peacefully achieved. Sturge wrote to him sharply: 'I have earnestly desired, that in any steps which Christians might take for the poor oppressed African race, they might not sacrifice principle for worldly expediency'. Buxton explained himself, but was met with Sturge saying that he could 'no longer satisfactorily co-operate with those who appear to me to act upon the principle that the end sanctifies the means.'

Sturge was a thorough Quaker and Buxton described himself as half a Quaker. Sturge kept to principles whatever the consequences and, although Buxton could not have been more unselfishly devoted to the good of the slaves, he put that before the ideal. The rift between the two was a great pity but did not continue without periods of calm, though it was almost entirely one-sided. For instance in 1838, shortly before the end of apprenticeship, Sturge called a large meeting of local representatives. It started with someone proposing a vote of criticism of Buxton for his policy. No one would second it and the meeting ended with Sturge himself asking to be allowed to take a message of thanks to Buxton for all that he had done. Nevertheless Sturge never quite forgave Buxton for agreeing to the £20,000,000 compensation.

By October 1835 Sturge and the UAS had set about a national campaign for the abolition of apprenticeship. Buxton and the Anti-Slavery Society surprisingly did nothing, waiting for the right moment to tackle the Government, lest they should weaken their stand on total freedom when the apprenticeship ended.

In March 1836 Buxton restored his reputation with the idealists to some extent by moving successfully for a Parliamentary committee of enquiry into how it was working. When however it reported in August its conclusions were ambiguous and Sturge decided to visit the West Indies with three other Quakers. He returned in May 1837 with news that fully justified another massive public campaign, published a scathing report and founded another new anti-slavery society with its own journal. Clearly the Liberation Act was being circumvented on a large scale in some areas by means of the Apprenticeship provisions. The Government was bombarded with propaganda. Petitions began to pour into Parliament from numerous local meetings, but they seem to have had little effect. A motion proposed in the House of Lords in February 1838 by Brougham, now Lord Brougham, was heavily defeated and attempts in the House of Commons were similarly frustrated by the Cabinet. The agitation continued unabated and *The Spectator* described the country as 'in convulsions' over the apprenticeship issue.

Finally in May 1838, in a thin House, the Government was humiliated by the passing of a motion abolishing apprenticeship. This was proposed by Sir Eardley Wilmot, as Buxton had been defeated in the 1837 election and was no longer an MP. He was however sitting in the gallery with friends and they cheered so vehemently that they were all ejected from the House for causing a disturbance!

This decision forced the Colonial Legislatures to comply and apprenticeship was soon ended. It was in fact dying out in one Colony after another, being abolished on their own initiative. News of the agitations in Britain probably helped considerably, creating the fear that London would impose an end on its own terms. In any case all domestic slaves were to be freed on August 1st 1838 and by July of that year it had almost finished.

Buxton probably lost his seat because in the previous few years he had upset many Anglicans by his close association with 'Dissenters', supporting the Irish Tithe Bill and the Bible Society and advocating other Church reforms. He wrote that 'the Church people are disaffected with me'. His support of Catholic Emancipation had upset many Free Church people also. He seems to have become more tactless. He had never cared much about his public reputation – he had had little chance – but his growing confidence led him into making some enemies outside Parliament rather unnecessarily. For instance on the Irish Tithes Bill, which greatly reduced the income of the Church of Ireland (from Catholic parishioners), he had said in the House:

> How has it been that truth itself, backed by a Protestant establishment, by a Protestant King, a Protestant parliament – that truth itself, so far from advancing, has not kept her ground against error? My solution of the question is, that we have resorted to force where reason alone could prevail....We have forgotten that there is something in the human breast – no base or sordid feeling – which makes men cleave with tenfold fondness to a persecuted religion. I charge the failure of Protestant truth in converting the Irish, upon the head of the Protestant ascendancy.
>
> Protestant ascendancy! It sounds well enough in English ears. It seems to mean no more than the Church under the peculiar protection of the State. But happy had it been for the Protestant Church, had Protestant ascendancy never been heard of – happy had it been, had we dared to present our truth to the Irish, not in arms, not in pomp, not decorated with the symbols of earthly power, but in that lowliness and gentleness which naturally belong to it.
>
> But I dare not trespass any longer on the House. I like the Bill and shall vote for it.[8]

It sounds as if he realised that this digression about the Protestant ascendancy was irrelevant to the arguments, which he had also set out, and he gave considerable offence by such remarks.

He had also refused to offer free beer and cash to voters as his rivals were doing. When told that he would not win unless he did so he replied: 'It might or it might not be my duty to get into Parliament, but it could not be my duty to corrupt the electors by beer and bank notes'. In fact his health had caused his wife and some of his friends to urge him not to stand, but he felt that that would be to run away from his responsibilities. As subsequent events showed his defeat was not a disaster for Africa, though in the short term he was sorely missed in Parliament. He had a unique influence there and he was still generally looked to for leadership on all slavery questions. Surprisingly his influence with the Cabinet did not seem to have diminished as he was still the spokesperson for a very powerful group of MPs and a huge group of voters. The absence from the House was a great relief to him physically and psychologically. He was able to settle down very soon, not to idleness, but to prolonged thought about what should be done for Africa.

He had of course agreed with Sturge that apprenticeship was a mistake, but had had to accept it. He had not expected it to work so badly and now acknowledged that he had been at fault in not pressing for an early end to it himself, though he did not admit any wrong motives for that. On hearing that the last apprenticeship had been ended (in Jamaica, Dominica, Bahamas and Trinidad) he wrote warmly congratulating Sturge for his important part in this result. He seems never to have borne any lingering resentment against any of his opponents, however sharply they had attacked him. It was a good example of his Christian generosity to others and willingness to admit it when he was proved wrong. To a friend he wrote: 'I must tell you that Sturge and his party, whom we thought all in the wrong, are proved to be all in the right.'

Sturge set about raising a new organisation on an international scale. Using the Birmingham Auxiliary as a base they called large meetings in Birmingham and then in London and, drawing in delegates from America and elsewhere, formed the 'British and Foreign Anti-Slavery Society'. This is the only one of the numerous societies that continues to this day, as 'Anti-Slavery International'. It has continued to monitor, campaign and try to influence Governments on slavery issues, but in the life time of Buxton its actual positive achievements were negligible. Buxton however had another and different idea developing in his mind and as Howard Temperley comments: 'It was Buxton, the conservative, who emerged as the true visionary.'[9]

CHAPTER 8

A Final Attack on the Continuing Slave Trade

BUXTON NOW BECAME the leader of a bold new approach to the problems of slavery. It was a far sighted vision and soon absorbed almost all his energies and in the end exhausted his health. He had always wanted to combine freedom with education and Christian teaching. One of the things that delighted him at this point was the success of the training institutions that he had helped to set up for Christian teachers in the schools. He was by no means the originator of the three pronged approach to the problems of Africa. Others had proposed in various ways one or more of the three 'Cs': Christianity, Commerce and Civilisation as partners in the advancement of what were seen as backward peoples. Sierra Leone had represented that vision, seeing civilisation as very much in the British model and believing that Christian teaching would bring such civilisation. Commerce had not been so important a hope there, though it was not absent from the plan and was at least implicit in it. Clarkson had constantly carried around with him a 'treasure chest' of African produce and artefacts to show how excellent was the culture and ability of the Africans. Without prosperous commerce it was clear that there was not likely long term to be good education, or the ability of the churches to find the money to be self financing, let alone to evangelise in neighbouring areas.

Buxton believed that good commerce would open the way for the spread of the gospel by indigenous evangelists, and so greatly further the evangelisation of Africa; but he gave a new emphasis to the whole vision by stressing also that to kill the Slave Trade there must be the substitution of wholesome trade that would be more profitable than selling people to the slavers. The Trade was keeping the whole continent in a chaos of tribal wars and preventing the development of any stable society. Therefore as soon as he was out of Parliament he began to think out a new approach to the problem of the continuing Slave Trade. One of his sons wrote:

> In the beginning of the summer of 1837, he walked into my room one morning, at an early hour, and sitting down on my bed-side, told me that he had been lying awake the whole night, reflecting on the subject of the Slave Trade, and that he believed that he had hit upon the true remedy for that portentous evil.

Now, Buxton said:

> Though strong external measures ought still to be resorted to, the deliverance of Africa was to be effected, by *calling out her own resources* (my emphasis).

Free now from the immediate pressures of Parliament he collected an enormous amount of material on the situation. His daughter Priscilla, with her husband Andrew Johnston, now joined him again in Norfolk, as Andrew had also lost his parliamentary seat. With the Cottage Ladies and, at last, a paid secretary they formed an extremely hard working team. He said that he thought he was working harder than he had done when in Parliament and harder than he had ever done since leaving College. By February 1838 he is writing: 'I only wish that the number of hours in each day were doubled, and the number of minutes quadrupled'. He wanted to show just how devastating was the effect of the continuing Slave Trade, how foul it was and also to collect evidence of the possibilities of commercial trade with Africa and the usefulness of its products as an alternative to the Trade. They pored over official statistics and figures to try to demonstrate beyond argument 'that the true way to abolish the Slave Trade would be to 'supplant it by lawful commerce'.

Working about twelve hours a day he prepared a 'Letter to Lord Melbourne' who was then the Prime Minister. Only 20 copies were printed as he wanted it at present to be a private statement. These he delivered in person to each of the relevant Ministers. He did not want the Cabinet to think that he was again going to try to pressurise them into action, but rather to persuade them by reasons into doing something themselves. They did not wish to be humiliated again as they had been over the apprenticeship. In any case there had been no doubt of their opposition to the Trade, even if they had hesitated about liberation.

Although he was no longer an MP Buxton still had extraordinary standing with the Cabinet and was in frequent consultation with them. The various officers at the Colonial Office in the rapidly changing Governments were extremely friendly. James Stephen (Jnr) the Permanent Under-Secretary and Lord Glenelg (Charles Grant Jnr), who was now the Colonial Secretary, were both sons of stalwart allies of Wilberforce in the Slave Trade abolition movement and fully supportive. Stephen in particular was a superb administrator and skillful drafter of memoranda for the Government and advisor of the right time and way to approach them. It was he who had drafted the Liberation Bill for Stanley in 1833, working almost non-stop for 48 hours to dictate the entire Bill of 66 clauses, when Stanley found he could not do it himself in the short time available. Stanley relied on this draft with confidence and the resulting Bill occupied 26 pages of the Statute Book.[1] Palmerston as Foreign Secretary was also sympathetic, though anxious lest Britain become too embroiled in Africa in ways that would divert energies, money and armed forces from other fields.

The 'Letter' was in fact a small book of 215 pages. He gave it to the Ministers just before the recess, urging them to read it when the parliamentary session was over. They did so and returned to discuss it with him. He had been horrified by what he and his team had discovered from all the official papers. In fact he was taken completely by surprise and shocked, as he had not kept up to date on the details of the Trade while he was occupied with liberation. Everyone had rather assumed that when Britain, who had been the largest player in the Trade, had stopped, then it must have declined greatly. To his horror and to the astonishment of the Government he showed that it had increased greatly since 1807. His booklet outlined many of the gruesome aspects of the Trade and the state in which it left large sections of Africa, aggravating tribal warfare and leaving devastated villages where there had been prosperous agriculture, quite apart from the suffering and death of so many on their way to the coast and across the Atlantic. Even the rather cynical Lord Melbourne commented that if half of what Buxton said was true it was a terrible situation.

While the British Navy had a squadron of 16 ships off the West Coast of Africa arresting slave ships and returning the slaves so captured to Sierra Leone or the West Indies, its effect was far smaller than he had realised. He showed that the very large expense of this squadron was achieving little. He estimated that 150,000 slaves a year were being landed in the Americas from West Africa by the Atlantic trade. Another 50,000 were being sent from the East Coast by the Arab traders. In the process, of course, huge numbers died before they reached the ships and on the journey. Only about one in three arrived alive and many of these were not well enough to survive the first months of 'seasoning'. For every three slaves surviving seven people had almost certainly died. The total he estimated was at least 500,000 a year killed or taken from Africa.[2] By comparison the squadron only caught about 8,000 a year to return to the coast. It was not unknown for slave ships, being chased by the Navy, to throw the slaves overboard so as to appear innocent and avoid arrest and confiscation. The cost of the current policies was huge, including 'bribes' to other countries to persuade them to stop. How much better it would be to spend this money on a programme that could cut off the Trade at its source, by making it more worthwhile for the African Chiefs to employ people to grow products that would fetch a good price in Europe. That would also bring profit to Britain and amongst other things reduce the dependence of Britain on American cotton, since it was known that cotton would grow well in West Africa and the supply of American cotton had proved unpredictable at times.

If Britain were to spend a comparable sum on establishing suitable commerce with the west coast it could cut off the Trade at its source. After an initial expenditure it would be self-financing, though some military presence would be needed at first to safeguard the scheme from slavers and others. The naval task force would need to be strengthened also, but the vision was far reaching and saw the possibility of a string of trading stations around the coast of Africa.

The Cabinet asked him not to publish the 'Letter' until they had more time to consider his practical remedies, so only the first part was published initially in 1839 under the title *The African Slave Trade*. It was in fact the first major treatment of the world-wide Trade and represented a massive piece of research on the little known Continent of Africa. Walls describes it as ' the first serious scholarly study of Africa'.[3] Buxton was one of the first people, other than slavers, to take a serious interest in the Continent. As was Buxton's policy, he quoted almost entirely from official documents that could not easily be refuted.

The last two chapters of the' Letter' had outlined practical measures that would need to be taken to bring about his strategy. The present policy he argued was in several ways only making things worse. It was putting up the value of slaves so that it was more worth while to export them. When a little later the entire work was published as *The African Slave Trade and its Remedy*[4] it made a widespread impact. It was 'a landmark in the Western understanding of Africa',[5] which to most people was little more that 'the Dark Continent'.

The Niger Expedition Proposed

Drastic new steps were needed. He proposed purchasing the island of Fernando Po from Spain as a base, and then sending an expedition up the river Niger to establish a model farm and trading posts well into the interior. He had ascertained that some at least of the chiefs were interested in legitimate trade. He had identified what he thought was probably the best location for a major trading and farming centre 300 miles up the Niger where it was joined by the Benue. One or more steam ships of shallow draft would be needed with a doctor and a botanist with appropriate seeds etc. His researches had identified many of the products that could be available for trade if produced by free labour: cotton, coffee, sugar, timber, drugs and minerals etc. Good trade he argued could increase the prosperity of both Africa and Britain.

One objection was the appalling health reputation of the West Coast. Buxton admitted that there would probably be some casualties, but he argued that, firstly, the crew and staff of the farms would as far as possible be Africans, recruited on the coast. Secondly, he believed that if those sent out from Britain were strong, healthy and clean living men, they would fare dramatically better than the riff-raff sailors and others who were the usual visitors to the coast. The unhealthy part he believed was chiefly, if not exclusively, on the coast and he planned a quick journey into the interior to a more healthy region. He believed (not quite correctly)

The great anti-slavery meeting in Exeter Hall, London to launch the Niger Expedition. Prince Albert is in the chair.

that there was a ridge of major hills not far from the coast, and there was evidence (quite correctly) that above a certain level fever was rare or absent. For once he failed in his research and of course he had never been there. He did not take into account the fact that very well staffed and reputable expeditions into the region, such as that led by Mungo Park, had suffered many casualties from fever. He also wrote off the experience of whites in Sierra Leone as due to the fact that it was on the coast and had poor soil. He had become so excited by his project and its genuine possibilities that he had not taken all his usual care about the health statistics. He may well have been influenced by the fact that Macaulay had survived several years at Sierra Leone quite well and John Clarkson had not suffered for a year there.

This was to prove his chief and fatal mistake. He had collected enormous details of possible products for trade and other features of the idea but he had little information about health and what he had had not been critically reviewed. The cause of Malaria was not known until 1897 and it was thought to be the result of the swamp air. Hence the name 'Mal-air-ia'. Also 'fever' included Yellow Fever, and the two were not distinguished. As a result quinine, which had been tried for Malaria, and had no effect on Yellow Fever, was little used. When it was, it was not used as a prophylactic but applied too late to be effective. No one had allowed for the incubation period of two or three weeks so there was no good remedy and mercury, which was used, was a poison! There were no effective remedies. The ships sent, he argued, could be constructed so as to reduce exposure to swamp air, by a system of air filtration. In any case, he claimed that the ways of living healthily in the tropics were now better understood including the value of fresh meat, exercise, cleanliness, sobriety and wearing of flannel next to the skin!

Motives and Over-confidence

Why then take the risks? As a country with a Christian culture and all its advantages, Britain had a responsibility to share its many good things with those who had never had the chance and the Slave Trade destroyed any chance of advancement. Buxton believed that his expedition would open the door to extensive trade and subsequently to missionary work. Africans he held were just as able as whites to develop their skills if they were given education and Christian teaching. In this Buxton was ahead of many. He was never condescending to people with less advantage than himself and that included Africans. Perhaps Abraham Plaistow, the gamekeeper of his childhood, had helped to teach him that they were often extremely wise.

He had, however, a great sense of the superiority of the Christian culture that Britain had been given by God's goodness, and the responsibility that that involved to share its good things, especially the Gospel on which he believed so much depended. He saw trade, education and Christianity as partners in bringing good to Africa. Also, for the benefit of those to whom money was what mattered, he claimed that in the long run it would be advantageous to the British economy. He was trying to meet the economic arguments against him with economic arguments. In some Victorians his approach became a condescending and patronising attitude. It was not so with Buxton, since he had such a high estimate of the capabilities of Africans if only given the chance to share some more of the benefits of a Christian culture. He cared of course also for the material and educational benefits in themselves. Historians often do not understand how the evangelical reformers of the nineteenth century could really care about social welfare, when they also wrote of the fact that the Gospel was by far the most important thing to give to anyone. Ford K. Brown, for instance, clearly fails here and by seizing on a few selective quotations goes so far as to say that they really did not care for the welfare of the slaves except as a means to an evangelistic outreach at home in Britain.

This is simply wrong.[6] The diaries of the evangelical reformers of both Wilberforce's generation and Buxton's clearly refute it. Buxton in particular was deeply upset by what he had found out about the human suffering involved. In fact he and the others of his evangelical outlook kept the two aspects (evangelism and social welfare) in a splendid partnership as both of value in themselves and a proper concern to all Christians. This is a balance that was sometimes lost in the early twentieth century and a tradition which evangelicals today would do well to note. To Buxton it was never an either/or, placing evangelism and social action in competition. Social action for the underprivileged was simply a plain Christian duty and was following New Testament instructions to seek to 'do good to all men'. There is no trace in the literature of the time that this was complicated, as it has sometimes been since, by talk about the Kingdom of God. That has contributed to the later reaction of some evangelicals from social action.

In the middle of all the excitement Buxton gave time to meet with the Bishop of London to discuss action for the acute needs of the suburb of Bethnal Green and the work of The London City Mission, of which he was now the Treasurer. He certainly maintained wide social concerns at home as well as abroad.

Was Buxton over-confident about his new idea? It seems that in some ways he was. He certainly gave much time to careful thought, research and prayer about it. He knew that without God's blessing it would not succeed. But having been, as he saw it, greatly blessed by God in carrying the liberation programme, he does seem to have been too easily convinced that this new vision would equally receive God's blessing and guidance. Like all who have been highly successful in one great venture there is an easy step into assuming that you cannot go wrong in the next one. Christians are as exposed to this danger as any one else. Although, like all the evangelical reformers of this period, he was constantly self critical as to his motives and his spiritual state and although he was consistently careless of the good opinion of other men, he seems to have begun to think that he could almost take the blessing of God for granted. His early conviction, often repeated to his sons, that 'with determination, hard work and perseverance a man could achieve anything – or almost anything', must have helped him into over confidence, now that he was older. He did not take as much care over the health issue as he did about the other aspects.

As for his personal motives, which he monitored repeatedly, he seems to have been splendidly free from the desire for status or fame. He several times wrote that he did not mind who got the credit for a programme so long as it did good. His ambition, in a good biblical tradition, was to use his gifts, status and money for service to God and humanity. He wanted to be useful and to serve in accordance with the view of work which he found in the New Testament, which he read constantly. This ideal of 'work as service' became deeply imprinted in many of the professions in Victorian times. If we laugh at it today, we suddenly realise our grave loss when it is replaced by the search only for money, status or reputation. Buxton was far from being alone in his aims, but it arose out of his Christian faith as it did with enough other people to influence a whole culture.

There was another danger sign in Buxton's programme. In the past he had relied for his support on fellow MPs and the huge popular agitation of ordinary people, although they were mostly middle class. He now set out to get the support of the socially great and famous for his new project. Perhaps it was necessary now that he was out of Parliament. He needed a lever to move the Government, but it was a dangerous policy. The historian of the Church Missionary Society notes that their similar drift towards seeking prestigious patronage about this time was a doubtful and dangerous development.[7] It became a snare to many Christian enterprises, leading them to give positions of influence to people not totally in sympathy with their aims.

The Expedition Launched

Buxton's 'Letter', given personally to all the members of the Cabinet, had achieved almost more than he had hoped. Called to the Colonial Office at the end of November 1838 he was asked to answer some questions about the idea. Spending much of the night at it he, Andrew Johnston and Stephen Lushington prepared a nine point proposal. It included an increase in the naval task force, the purchase of Fernando Po island (Spain in the end refused to sell) and an expedition well up the Niger to make treaties with the chiefs, agreeing to establish trade if they would give up the Slave Trade, and to set up a model farm. Buxton was received by the Prime Minister, Melbourne, the Foreign Secretary, Palmerston, and Lord John Russell the Home Secretary[8] as if they needed his help to work out a proposal that would satisfy the 'humanitarians' and help them to meet opposition on other issues. He could not exactly dictate the terms of the planned expedition but they were obviously eager to put out his ideas as their own, if they could be made practicable. He had done the research and no other way of tackling the Trade was in sight. Since 1807 they had been trying with little or no effect. Everyone was agreed that the Trade was vile and ought to be stopped.

Buxton and his friends were clearly motivated by moral principles. They had to persuade the Government, and others to whom that was not so important, to support the programme. As in most such campaigns the number of really committed supporters is not large enough to carry the day without persuading others to join them in the cause for a mixture of motives. Those who hope to succeed in a moral campaign in politics without asking others from different outlooks to join them are rarely successful. Certainly both the campaign on the Trade and the campaign for liberation could not have succeeded on the strength of the relatively small number of strongly Christian enthusiasts in Parliament. To us it is surprising how quickly the Government now came to join Buxton's project. Their motives, and the motives of other influential people who came in, no doubt ranged from pure commercial speculation to moral concern. The Government of Lord Melbourne was also not too secure and they could not risk crossing the very considerable body of moral concern in and out of Parliament. Certainly there is no reason to think that Melbourne was much moved by the moral issues. Nevertheless it was not long before there was every expectation that the Government would find the necessary funds for an exploratory journey up the Niger and the establishment, well away from the coast, of a model farm. They had adopted the idea with some enthusiasm, knowing that the country was wholeheartedly against the Trade. The idea of using trade and education to develop Africa was far from new. What was new was the vision of these as the final blow to the Slave Trade and slavery itself. That made it attractive to a far wider public and therefore to the Government. In Dec. 1838 Buxton wrote:

> I have had many interviews with members of the Cabinet. [and again a few days later] I was ushered into the presence of Lord Glenelg, muttering to myself, 'O God, give me good speed this day'. I soon found that my nine points had worked admirably. They were formally discussed in the Cabinet. Glenelg intimated that the ministers were unanimous, and that they had resolved, with some modifications, to act upon them. I did not sleep well, who could expect it after such a day; after finding that it was intended to realise my most intense desires.

The Government would produce a considerable sum of money but could not do so before the end of the financial year. Buxton and his friends agreed to find a proportion from private subscriptions in the City. The Cabinet agreed that there should be two ships to be accompanied by a frigate.

There is a recent and very well researched study of the expedition by Professor Howard Temperley.[9] As he had access to the detailed diaries of the ships officers etc. the whole story can be followed there. Our concern here however has to be mainly with Buxton's part in it and the ultimate effect of what, at least on the surface, looked like a spectacular failure. It was Buxton's last great effort.

Buxton's book had made many people realise, as they had not done before, that the Trade was continuing on a very big scale, that its horrors were as great as ever and that unless something new was done it would continue unabated. This discovery had been a shock to Buxton and was new and shocking to the populace in general. It created a massive body of support for his proposal.

He had hoped that an expedition could sail in 1839, but it was found that there was no suitable ship available with a shallow draught and steam powered. Steam powered ships were in any case still few and it had to be able to burn coal or timber as need arose. Ships would have to be built specially. Clearly delay was inevitable. The Navy however were not averse to having extra steam ships available for future use and it now became clear that there should be two or three such ships. Lairds of Birkenhead were commissioned to build two. Buxton, Sam Hoare and others guaranteed to find part of the cost if the Government in the end failed to pay. That made it possible to start work.

Other problems also arose and the plan began to attract publicity and also opposition. Buxton and Lushington then created a cross-party group to be known as 'The Patrons of Africa'. It included W.E. Gladstone, Samuel Gurney (Hannah's very wealthy younger brother), Lord Ashley (the future Lord Shaftesbury of reforming fame), the Bishop of London and others who he described as 'Whig, Tory and Radical, Dissenter, Low Church, High Church'. Gladstone asked about the health problem and Buxton had to admit that he was not fully briefed on that but would set further research in hand. He asked the team at Northrepps to go into it further as well as to pursue some other questions. At this point, however, one of the Cottage Ladies, his sister Sarah Maria Buxton, died suddenly and that research never seems to have been very thoroughly carried out.

It then emerged that many of the keen liberationists in the Agencies led by Sturge were against the scheme. This was because they were Quakers, and therefore pacifists, and could not support the possible use of force to protect the farms and settlements against slavers and others and certainly the use of an increased naval force arresting slavers. Sturge and his allies believed that the real solution was to be through persuading other nations to stop their Trade. In fact Brazil and Cuba were now the chief importers from West Africa, and they were hard to influence, though they were helped by Portuguese and Spanish ships. Brazil was importing nearly 100,000 each year.[10] Buxton's scheme was in their view not only wrongly dependent on the use of force; it was also impracticable. As long as there was a continuing demand for slaves they believed that there would be people who would find ways to get round the obstacles put in their way. They did not always allow for the fact that in none of the other countries concerned was there such a powerful humanitarian lobby both inside and outside their Parliaments and able to some extent to twist the arms of their Governments. Their policy was therefore less practical than it seemed to be from the home base.

Over the following years Sturge and his allies in the Anti-Slavery Society proposed a series of measures to persuade other countries to abolish slavery. They called the first World Anti-Slavery Convention in London in 1840, including a group of 43 representatives from the USA, and set about stirring up a world-wide agitation for the elimination of slavery, but their policies made very little practical difference. Anti-slavery people in the USA were very divided as to the right ways of proceeding and this delayed action there. Meanwhile trading continued on a considerable scale, in the case of Cuba until 1867.[11] Unofficial trading continued even after that.

Sturge has been accused of a certain jealousy about Buxton's leadership, but that is probably unfair. His views on the Niger Expedition were not altogether unreasonable. Both men were consistent in their own terms. Sturge and his Quaker allies were consistent pacifists and Buxton planned to use the Navy and a small military force to protect the settlements. Sturge, for reasons that are not clear, wrote to *The Times* criticising the proposed expedition. The *Times* was an influential and strongly Tory paper, with a circulation of nearly 60,000. It joined in criticism of the plan with ridicule, including:

> The absurdity of a handful of European adventurers expecting, as if by an enchanter's wand, to change the face of the great African continent, and stop the slave trade, on the principles of political economy surpasses anything which the imagination of Swift was able to conceive.[12]

Others attacked the project scornfully in letters to the Press and even spoke up against it at public meetings called to raise support for it. The Government however was committed to the expedition and if they were told how divided the humanitarians were they did not seem to bother.

His book published and the expedition being secure and firmly a Government project, Buxton followed his wife to Italy for a break, where she had been sent for the sake of her health. Here, however, he became seriously ill again and his return was delayed until he was fit to travel. He corresponded constantly with Lushington, who was in charge of operations while he was away. His son remarks that for the first time he became a really good correspondent! He only returned in May 1840.

A FINAL ATTACK ON THE CONTINUING SLAVE TRADE   121

Meanwhile a massive public meeting had been organised for June 1st. By frequent correspondence he took the major part in the plans, including the proposal to invite Prince Albert, the Queen's husband, to be present and speak for the expedition. Buxton was widely seen as the man behind the meeting. Crowds of the 'great and good' attended, including the Duke of Norfolk (the premier Peer of the realm) two Marquises, seven Earls and numerous Lords and Bishops etc. The Prince made his first ever public speech, supporting the venture. He had only been married to Queen Victoria for four months and what he would say was watched with the greatest interest. The Duke of Norfolk led the platform party, which included Sir Robert Peel the Leader of the Opposition in Parliament, several other MPs and Bishops and a number of Peers. A motion to create 'The African Civilisation Society' was passed with enthusiasm and 70 Vice-Presidents were appointed including 3 Archbishops, 16 Bishops, 5 Earls and 20 other Peers. A smaller executive Committee was to be chaired by Buxton himself. It was he who was generally regarded as the leader of the anti-slavery cause and the architect of this new and far ranging vision for the spread of civilisation and Christianity in Africa. The Missionary Societies were well represented as they were enthusiastic and hoped that continental Africa would be opened up. As yet very little in the way of missionary work been achieved in Africa apart from the coastal areas, including the efforts in Sierra Leone, where the population was dominated by returned slaves, including the remarkable Anglican catechist Samuel Crowther. He was sent by CMS to be the African chaplain on the expedition.

Soon after the meeting Buxton was called to the Home Office and went fearing another Government hindrance, only to be offered a Baronetcy. After some hesitation he accepted. His semi-Quaker principles made him doubtful and he made no fuss of it, but even his Quaker relatives urged him to accept as it would strengthen the cause.

Two paddle steamers (screw propulsion was still uncommon) were built specially with retractable keels and a most elaborate apparatus for filtering the 'swamp air' before it entered the interior of the ships, as that was thought to be the cause of 'fever'. They were named the *Wilberforce* and the *Albert*. Each drew only 4¾ feet but were armed with guns and small arms. A smaller ship the *Soudan* had a draught of only 3 feet. The crews were all volunteers on double naval pay in view of the dangers. The officers were all white, but 28 of the 95 seamen were black and it was intended to take on more Africans at Sierra Leone and Liberia to work the farms. In all there were in the end 150 Europeans and as many Africans in the party, though they started with half that number. The only non-naval personnel were missionaries, agriculturalists and scientists and they were to be paid for by Buxton and his friends. When the ships were ready they were moved to Deptford and then to Woolwich, where they were visited by Prince Albert, who was well impressed, and of course by Buxton and others. A widely observed day of prayer was called and a farewell service at Woolwich before they set out. The Press also became generally positive and enthusiasm ran high. They finally sailed in January 1841, but did not cross the bar into the Niger until August, having called at Sierra Leone, Gold Coast (now Ghana) and Liberia to take African crew on board. These included re-captive slaves to act as interpreters, since many knew the languages of the area.

So far everything seemed to be going well, though they lost one man through fever at that point. Two others had fallen overboard earlier. They went up the river making treaties with the chiefs, who

The ship Wilberforce. *It was a paddle steamer, powered by both sail and steam.*

agreed, at least in theory, to cease the Trade in return for the commerce that would follow. This delayed them and the idea of a quick journey to the interior proved impossible. Then fever began to appear in the crew and one after another became seriously ill and unable to work. Deaths began to increase. The doctors treated them with mercury until, mercifully, the supply was lost overboard as it was being transferred from one ship to another. They reached the point of the junction of the Niger and Benue, 300 miles from the coast, where Buxton had planned to put the model farm, bought land and settled a party in charge of one Alfred Carr, a young Trinidadian, who had been recruited in England for the purpose. Sickness however now struck almost all the crew. At one point the *Wilberforce* had only three officers and ten crew fit for duty. The commander and all the engineers were too sick to work, so the geologist and one of the doctors had to work the engines with the help of a book on board. The *Soudan* was sent down river loaded with the sick to take them to Fernando Po.

Deaths multiplied and before long all the ships had to descend the river to allow the crew to recover on Fernando Po or Ascension Island. When after a while the *Wilberforce* was sent back up the river to find out how the settlement and farm were going on, they found that Alfred Carr had been murdered when on an expedition away from the farm, that little work was being done and that the cotton seed brought out from England had failed. Local seed seemed promising, but the soil was not specially fertile there. It was decided to close the settlement and the ships returned to England, to the relief of the crews. In the end 53 of the original 150 white personnel died, 44 of them from fever. Others were to suffer long term damage to their health and the gains seemed almost negligible. In the longer term there were considerable gains but at the time they were not evident. It is true that they had explored and mapped the Niger, of which little had been known. This gave the Missionary Societies help and they took up the challenge to develop their work in West Africa. This was not without further very heavy losses amongst the missionaries. But missionary casualties were accepted as inevitable in those times. There was however a fresh emphasis on local leadership and when Samuel Crowther was made a Bishop he had great influence in a wide area of West Africa. There were other important long term benefits, as discussed later, but at the time they were not evident and the whole expedition seemed to have been a total disaster.

When the first news reached England and told of some casualties, Buxton persisted in hope. After all if it had been a war of aggression there would have been casualties. A whole army of thousands had recently disappeared in Afghanistan. When he heard that casualties were mounting, including one of the commanders who was a personal friend, he was deeply upset. As the news got worse and the Press attacked the whole project with ridicule he felt crushed. He could not work out why God had allowed this disaster. He still believed that good would come out of it but it was a shattering blow to him and his supporters. His health had been poor for some years and the repeated blows crushed even his resilience. His last public acts were to attend a meeting to wind up the African Civilisation Society and then to report in person to Prince Albert on the whole story. He remained at Northrepps, with a break to 'take the waters' at Bath for his health, and only a very few visits to London. He rose very early in the mornings and gave a lot of time to prayer, saying that if he could not do much else he could at least do that. He found great pleasure in his tree plantations and was reported as particularly happy that they gave employment to local people on previously uncultivated land (incidentally at a very good wage). At one point he was employing 93 men at a time when unemployment was high.

He sent apologies for not attending the Anti-Slavery Convention organised by Sturge, writing: ' I can no longer unite with you in fighting: but my prayer to God is that He would stand by all those who are engaged in this holy enterprise to put down these iniquities'. He said that he still hoped to be able to do something for Africa but commented: 'no matter who is the instrument, so long as there be successful labourers for God, for Christ, and for man, especially for heathen man'.

On one Sunday Samuel Crowther, who had been brought over to England, preached an 'excellent sermon' in Overstrand Church and Buxton was much encouraged by this evidence that his confidence in the ability of Africans had been demonstrated so well in that sphere. Crowther was presented at court to the Queen, immaculately dressed in British style, and impressed people that an African could fit into the British scene and culture so well. It reinforced the idea that African culture could be transformed into the Western mould! In the long run that may have undermined the stress on African leadership in Africa, but at the time it gave confidence to trust the African leadership, especially as the health hazards for Europeans were so formidable. Crowther was actually an outstanding student of West African languages and culture, which he valued and tried to develop critically but constructively. Sadly most of his carefully collected materials were lost in a house fire and never replaced. It seems that as foreign missionaries took over much of the leadership of the churches in the second half of the century a good deal of the emphasis on local leadership was lost. If Buxton had lived longer he might have been able to correct that to some extent by his confidence in Africans.

Buxton's death

Buxton roused himself to correspond with the Government on issues about which he felt strongly. He urged them, for instance, that they should maintain a duty on slave-grown sugar from Brazil and Cuba and on another occasion that they drop a plan for the compulsory emigration to the West Indies of re-captured slaves returned to Sierra Leone. This he argued would weaken the education and training programme in Sierra Leone which was producing some fine leaders for education and missionary work in West Africa as a whole. Here he was proved right. Fourah Bay College became a flagship educational establishment for Africa and for its churches (see pp61 and 141).

His health, however, declined steadily. He maintained correspondence, mainly on African and slavery affairs, and he received visitors, but he suffered periods of extreme fatigue and forgetfulness with intervals of recovery into greater energy, activity and clarity of mind. Sometimes he was even in a wheel-chair. His wife gave him continual support as she remained well and in fact lived serenely to the age of 88 at Northrepps, outliving all her eleven brothers and sisters except the youngest, and surrounded by her numerous grandchildren and their Gurney, Fry and Hoare cousins. He finally died on 19th February 1845 aged 59 at Northrepps and was buried in the ruined part of Overstrand Church, where his wife was also buried when she died. The church has since been extended over the grave and has some good memorials to him and to others of the family.

It was said by his friends that the failure of the expedition killed him, though 59 was not a bad age for his generation and he had repeatedly been a very sick man. His funeral was attended by a large crowd of the fishermen and ordinary country labourers from the villages round about, where he was greatly respected and loved. That was probably as he would have wished, though it contrasts strikingly with Wilberforce's magnificent funeral in Westminster Abbey, attended by two Royal Dukes and numerous leaders of national life.

It was obviously the very public failure of the Niger Expedition that resulted in an ambiguous memory of him in Britain and the eclipse of his name from many lists of well known nineteenth century reformers. Also many of the Quakers and other idealists never forgave him for making concessions to the Government so as to get the Act through. *The Times* even managed to attack him in their obituary notice saying:

> With regard to the disastrous Niger expedition....He was the mainspring of that lamentable undertaking....his maladies grievously aggravated by the regrets and disappointments which attended his latest labours: thus probably his life was shortened by the erroneous estimate which he formed of his qualifications as a statesman and reformer.[13]

Time was to show that in fact the Niger expedition had accomplished a great deal, at least indirectly, as explored in the next chapter. Those who remembered his Herculean efforts and success on the behalf of the slaves however raised a considerable sum, much of it in pennies and half-pennies from ex-slaves, for the memorial in Westminster Abbey, almost next to that of Wilberforce. Prince Albert contributed and altogether about 50,000 people gave towards it. In the West Indies and in West Africa he was greatly mourned and remembered with gratitude. In Sierra Leone also a considerable public subscription was raised for the bust in the Cathedral which was erected in his memory there.

The memorial inscription in Westminster Abbey includes:

> Of dauntless courage and untiring energy he was early led by the love of God to devote his powers to the good of man. In Parliament he laboured
> > For the improvement of Prison Discipline
> > For the amendment of the Criminal Code

For the suppression of Suttee in India
For the Liberation of the Hottentots in South Africa
and above all
For the emancipation of eight hundred thousand slaves in the British Dominions
In this last Righteous Enterprise, after ten years of arduous conflict a final Victory was given to him and his co-adjutors, "By the Good hand of our God" on the memorable 1st of August, 1834.

The energies of his mind were afterwards concentrated on a great attempt to extinguish the Slave Trade in Africa by the substitution of Agriculture and Commerce and by the civilising influence of the Gospel.

This monument is erected by his friends and fellow-labourers at home and abroad assisted by the grateful contributions of many thousands of the African race.

Buxton's Character and Priorities

Professor Andrew Walls, who has studied him in depth, describes him as 'rather an engaging character'.[14] He was not a complicated person. There was a certain straightforwardness about him so that people seem to have known where they stood in relation to him, even when they disagreed. He was never devious or even very subtle. In many ways he was a very natural country gentleman, delighting in his family and friends and teaching his children to take great pleasure in nature and the discoveries of science as those were made known to the public. He was devoted to his wife and children and they responded with warm devotion to him. He was also the centre of a wider circle of relatives and friends whom he supported generously with time and money when needed.[15]

He might today be thought of as something of an environmentalist; giving a lot of attention to his plantations, voting in Parliament for the Acts that led to the establishment of the RSPCA, even when it meant cancelling other engagements,[16] and re-introducing the Capercaillie into Scotland. At the same time he combined this with shooting as a sport (though of course the game was food). He saw no inconsistency in that and took great pleasure in the countryside and its beauties and in unusual birds and animals, some of which roamed round his land. When in Norfolk he had often gone out riding for an hour before breakfast just to enjoy it and the scenery. When he was not excessively busy and over tired he romped with his children and their cousins. In the middle of a very busy period he is writing to a small child about his pet rabbit. No childish pleasures were beneath him. He was however very keen on the children's education. Most unusually for the times he had sent his daughter Priscilla away to boarding school, when she asked to be like her brothers. As a result she had a far better education than most young ladies, including her Gurney aunts, who had as usual been educated entirely at home. In the end he benefited considerably from this when she became virtually his secretary. He cared greatly for education generally. At the brewery he insisted that all the staff should learn to read. He saw literacy as a key element in the raising of his staff and the ex-slaves to a better life.

He had his own idiosyncrasies, but they did not prevent his being widely respected and loved by people of all classes. As a man of his times, and who is not, he accepted the class structure of society without question, but he related easily to people at all levels in a natural way. This was shown particularly in his attitude to Africans. He really believed in the capacity of all kinds of people to rise to the top if given the chance. When for instance he spoke at one of the CMS Annual Meetings he obviously enjoyed quoting from one of Cicero's letters to Atticus:

> The then Chief Orator of Rome, writing to a friend, said, 'There is a slave-ship arrived in the Tiber, laden with slaves from (an obscure) Island ; but' he adds, 'don't take one of them: they are not fit for use'. That island was Britain! Yet Rome has found her rival in Britain. May not a day arrive when the sons of these degraded Africans will run with you the race of religion and morality, and even outstrip you in the glorious career.[17]

He was far ahead of his time in this and it arose from his Christian belief in all people as equally God's special creation and therefore of equal value to God and unique value to us – a view which he shared of course, at least theoretically, with most Christians. It was to him, however, a deeply held conviction, as it was with most of the evangelical reformers. To treat slaves as property or animals was outrageous, as the fighters against the Trade had argued, but he added his conviction that they could be equal socially and educationally.

He was quite widely read, not only in the classical literature that was the staple education of schools and Universities, but Earlham had taught him to read much more widely and to take pleasure in poetry and in literary style. He started in London, and continued in Norfolk, 'reading evenings' when anyone of his circle was encouraged to read a poem, or other piece of their choice or their own composition, to a gathered company of local and family contacts. In Parliament he studied with care the style of his models and his dislikes, setting out some principles of what went down well in the House. Writing to a friend about style he recommended him to read Cicero, Quintilian, Chesterfield's and Junius's letters, Demosthenes, South's sermons and *The Spectator*.

In public his image was that of a deeply committed man. He was inflexible in following the causes that met the needs of the disadvantaged, so that the liberation struggle and the Niger Expedition became consuming passions. He did not really enjoy being in Parliament, but he felt a responsibility to do what he could there, as he had the gifts and opportunity and found too few people willing to put themselves out for causes that helped those in need – even when they agreed that something ought to be done by someone. For such causes, which he saw in terms of disadvantaged *people*, he repeatedly worked himself into illness as he knew that they could only be won by carefully sifted facts. In 1818 he had written to J.J. Gurney:

> I am, I believe, rather absurd; but I hold a doctrine, to which I owe – not much, indeed but all the little success I ever had, – viz. that with ordinary talents and extraordinary perseverance, all things are attainable.

He knew that he was not as able as some of the other MPs but he also knew that he could work harder and be more persistent than most people. He wrote:

> energy, invincible determination – a purpose once fixed, then death or victory. That quality will do anything that can be done in this world: and no talents, no circumstances, no opportunities, will make a two-legged creature a man without it.

That does not mean that he approved the developing tendency to what became British Imperialism. He disliked the military spirit and his pleasure at the retreat of the British Army in South Africa (p102) shows an attitude that might surprise us in a Victorian MP. He was always on the side of the underdog, so long as it did not lead to the total breakdown of good order. His parliamentary career made him sometimes hated and sometimes admired, but he tried not to mind so long as the disadvantaged gained something.

His daily reading of the Bible and considerable thought about its teaching as it applied to himself, saved him from the temptations of pride and selfish ambition to a great extent, though he was aware of the temptation and would not have professed never to have been attracted by it or fallen for it.

In the end, after his success on liberation, he seems to have fallen for a certain over-confidence, and as he grew confident he became more strident in some of his views. He was however deeply committed to the causes that he felt he could advance and he sacrificed much of his energy, health, money and home pleasures for those concerns. Above all he was a Christian who tried to put his faith into practice. He knew that he did not always succeed but he saw himself as a forgiven sinner, and so had confidence in God and could trust Him through thick and thin.

CHAPTER 9

Long Term Results of Liberation and the Niger Expedition

IT IS IMPORTANT TO try to assess the longer term results of both of these two great programmes, because, in the long run, they affected millions of people. They dominated Buxton's concerns from 1821 to his death in1845, but one must not neglect his role in South Africa and in the penal code, the conditions in prisons, his work in education and his work to help the poor in London in various ways. It could never be said of him that he cared exclusively for people abroad to the neglect of issues at home. He was not, however, a member of the Government. He was a working (but unpaid) MP and like others had responsibilities to his business and his family etc. He never held a Cabinet appointment or shared directly in the overall responsibilities of government. He concentrated on those issues at home and abroad to which he felt he could make some effective contribution. He never attempted to get deeply involved in those social reforms that were being advanced in his later years by his younger colleague, the evangelical Lord Ashley (1801-1885 becoming the Earl of Shaftesbury in 1851). Liberation and the Niger Expedition were Buxton's two greatest projects and are his chief legacy.

The Results of Liberation

Opponents of liberation had predicted all kinds of disasters. Slave owners in the United States continued to put the worst possible interpretation on the results, so as to warn of the dangers of liberation there.

The most important gains were not measurable in economic terms. The whole culture of the Colonies was changed for the better. Firstly, stable married life became possible as families could no longer be split up at auction. As a result the number of registered marriages increased rapidly and couples could be sure to live on the same plantation. Ex-slaves could now own land and homes and work on both to produce improvements. Before long some were members of the local legislature. They could put their children into school, and there was no danger that they would be sold off. Their evidence in court had to be taken like that of anyone else. When apprenticeship ended they could no longer be subject to arbitrary punishments if they did not work. They were citizens, not property that could be exploited for the pleasure or gain of planters[1] and the often remote plantation owners, who had lived in luxury in England. The latter it is true lost out to some extent, but they were rich people who were not driven to hardship. The slaves could settle down to several generations of peaceful and free life under the relatively safe and well regulated rule of the British Government. The British Flag gave a reasonably just society and security and freedom from war as well as from slavery.

Secondly education, and particularly Christian education, became the rule. Children and adults could now learn to read and literacy and numeracy became common. A community that had recently come out of a mixture of diverse animistic beliefs in Africa was now able to find coherence and unity in understanding and adopting a broadly Christian culture and outlook. The planters had as a rule vigorously discouraged both education and Christian teaching. As has been noted, Buxton foresaw the opportunity and had prepared for it with his teacher training programme in the year before actual liberation. With others he also followed this up afterwards. A recent reminder of this was seen on British TV in 1998 when pictures of the *Windrush* immigrants to Britain in 1948 were shown and their broadly Christian outlook was explored. In 1999 a student leader in Jamaica wrote of 'the pervasive Christian influence in the country' and noted that 'the Christian infrastructure is dominant'. This of course owes much to the valiant efforts of the Missionary Societies both before and following liberation and the great influence of prominent indigenous preachers over the years. The latter included some free blacks from North America who had been influenced by the revivalism of the second 'Great Awakening' there and arrived as zealous and very effective ex-slave evangelists in the 1830s and 40s.[2] The result was a coherent moral and religious consensus, which created a stable society.

It had been widely predicted that freed slaves would refuse to work and that apart from other disasters there would be a dramatic decline in sugar production, which in turn would lead to the collapse of the whole West Indian economy. Considering that the slaves' working day had often been 14 hours (up to 19 at harvest time), with a whip to keep them going, some decline in working hours was inevitable and desirable. The liberation party's hope that free labour would quickly produce more than slave labour was not proved altogether correct, although some increase in sugar export followed in the first two years. That was not continued and they were a little disappointed in the short term.

Nevertheless the economy did not at all collapse, for reasons given below. In Antigua and Bermuda where apprenticeship was not adopted and slaves were immediately freed, sugar production and other trade increased very well. The same was true in some other islands, but in Jamaica and Demerara in particular there were considerable difficulties, in both partly at least because of the very bad relations between planters and slaves over the years.

Where there was uncultivated land still available, especially in Jamaica, many slaves moved from the plantations and set up their own smallholdings, coming in to the plantations for work as much as they needed to supplement their own produce. This was a great gain to the ex-slaves but did not always suit the planters so well. The ex-slaves may have worked as hard as before, but a slice of it was on their own land and houses. The planters later began to import labour from Asia in the form of volunteer, officially free but 'indentured' workers; but this cannot have had much effect until the 1860s.[3]

Slave owners in the southern USA and planters in the British Colonies, who could no longer claim that liberation would lead to bloodshed, mounted a considerable outcry about the evil effects of liberation on the economy. Some of the claims made were clearly false[4] and some of the claims on the other side were probably exaggerated, but in general the economy of the Colonies soon settled down to being reasonably prosperous. There were still a good many in Britain who did not believe that Africans could compare with whites and wanted to hear the worst. It is not unfair to compare the lot of the ex-slaves and their descendants in the West Indies with the lot of the slaves in USA, even after liberation there. In the USA good education was greatly delayed and a culture of blacks as second class citizens was very difficult to eradicate, even into the second half of the Twentieth Century. The British West Indies became a far better place for ex-slaves, even though British capital investment tended to move from the region into India and the Far East or parts of Africa, so that economic development was slow.

Charles Buxton published an article in the Edinburgh Review in 1859 on *The Results of Emancipation*, which is almost fully reprinted in the 1882 'New Edition' of his 'Memoirs' of his father.[5] As an MP he had easy access to government reports and could insist on seeing other papers. He treats several issues, but was chiefly concerned to reply to those who still claimed that liberation had been an economic disaster for the Colonies and that the slaves were lapsing into idleness. He shows that, whereas before emancipation the population was 'rapidly being killed off', after that date it began to increase again. His figures are a decline of 60,219 out of 558,194 on the eleven islands that gave returns in the twelve years before liberation. In the twelve years after liberation ten of these islands alone recorded an increase of 54,074. Secondly, sugar production had in fact risen considerably by 1856 (the last year he seems to have figures) whereas, not surprisingly, it had been declining in the last few years before liberation as the slave population was declining. Exports to Britain were up and there was additional new trade to USA and Australia, which there had not been before 1834. It was true that when in 1847 the taxes giving preference to Colonial sugar had been removed there had been a short lived decline. Up to that date sugar from other countries had been at a commercial disadvantage.[6] This decline had been seized on by the critics and given considerable publicity, but it was soon remedied and the then improved situation received far less notice because it did not raise protests from the sugar trade in the press and in Parliament.

No one should suggest that the transition was without difficulties, or that there were not instances of misuse of liberty. But generally the advances were spectacular and on a grand scale. The racial snobbery of some white people began to be changed a little as the 'free peasantry', which Buxton had so much looked forward to, showed itself quite capable of success.

By no means all Christians shared Buxton's confidence in Africans. Many had only met blacks as uneducated slaves, or heard of them in that sort of status. Hurrel Froude, for instance, one of the leaders of the High Church 'Oxford Movement' was violently hostile to both Buxton and to blacks. He wrote that he had: 'no love for the niggers' because they 'concentrated in themselves all the Whiggery, dissent, cant and abomination that has been ranged on their side'. Even more pointedly he wrote : 'I cannot get over my prejudice against the niggers; every one I meet seems to me like an incarnation of the whole Anti-Slavery Society and Fowell Buxton at its head'.[7] Howse comments that, without prejudice to the good that the Oxford Movement may have done in other areas, it would have been a disaster if its social policies had ruled the Churches in the first half of the nineteenth century, rather than that of the evangelicals, who, thankfully, led the way at that time. Buxton and his allies were ahead of their time and would have been delighted, but not at all surprised, to be told that the Secretary General of the United Nations in the 1990s was Kofi Annan, a West African, and educated in Ghana, and that one of the most respected political leaders world wide and a Nobel Prize winner was a South African Black, Nelson Mandela.

David Livingstone (1813-1873) is recorded as finding that in his travels in East and Southern Africa he met with the report amongst Africans that there was one white nation that cared for the good of their people and he could build on that good will. The ripples had evidently spread widely.

The Results of the Niger Expedition

There was an important incidental benefit of the Niger expedition that is picked up by Temperley.[8] Almost the only three whites who did not suffer from fever were the three doctors. At least one of them, Dr Thomas Thomson, and perhaps all three, were taking quinine daily. This must have been because they hoped it might help against 'fever'. Quinine had generally been abandoned, because the strength of the available drug varied wildly and it was not taken until the symptoms appeared, which was too late for it to be very effective. Only when the cause of malaria was discovered in 1879 did it become clear that there was a considerable incubation period. Also 'fever' included Yellow Fever against which quinine was totally ineffective. When Thomson returned to England and stopped taking it he had a mild attack of fever. He wrote up this experience in *The Lancet* in 1846. This led in 1848 to a general recommendation to all British military and naval personnel in West Africa to use quinine. The use of mercury, emetics and bleeding, which had been tried on the expedition, were also discouraged as worse than useless. These recommendations must have saved many lives in the following years.

On the surface the Niger expedition was a total disaster and achieved nothing. Certainly it is hard to measure the results, but after a while it emerged that it had had very important benefits, which were to last for a long time. The expedition greatly expanded knowledge of Africa in the public mind. Indeed before that more was known about the animals than the peoples or the conditions, except to a few slavers. *The Times*, consistently with its then scornful attitude to nearly all philanthropy, ridiculed the failure as 'the schemes of dreamers' which were 'sufficient to consign African philanthropy to everlasting ridicule and scorn'.[9] The historian of the C.M.S. wrote:

> *The Times* was triumphant; the very name of the Niger Expedition became a byword and a proverb to express hopeless failure.... The promoters did not all lose heart: they held another meeting to which Lord John Russell, now leader of the Opposition.... had the courage to come and speak, boldly asserting, against all cavils, the soundness of Buxton's schemes, and prophesying that the failure was only temporary.[10]

That sort of situation no doubt contributes considerably to the fact that Buxton is relatively little known. Charles Dickens took up the theme, ridiculing the aims of the expedition on several occasions, notably in *Bleak House* with his caricature of Mrs Jellyby, who neglected her children for the sake of helping the settlement at Borrioboola-Gha on the left bank of the Niger! Outside Christian circles and ex-slave communities Buxton's name was not held in the honour he deserved for a considerable while. He was not without defenders at the time. *The Morning Chronicle*, for instance, issued a vigorous riposte to *The Times*, expressing its 'disgust' at the 'insults',[11] and Dickens was attacked for his caricature. Nevertheless inevitably considerable damage was done to Buxton's public standing.

The casualties were serious. It should however be said that secular explorers were not being vilified but praised for deeds of daring that cost lives and benefited no one in particular, and the military cheerfully accepted massive loss of life from diseases, such as cholera and dysentery in India, as the price of conquest. What gave hostages to the cynics was the great public send off and the involvement of secular authorities such as senior politicians and Prince Albert at Exeter Hall.

If *The Times* thought philanthropy towards Africa a dead issue now, Christian leaders were not put off efforts to develop the vision that the expedition had represented. The Missionary Societies enlarged their work, often giving leadership roles in a previously very unusual way to Africans, as the official report on the expedition to the CMS Committee recommended. They had gained from the expedition a lot of information about the previously little explored river Niger and Samuel Crowther, who it will be remembered had been chaplain on the expedition, now knew the lower 300 miles of it quite well. Before long he had established a chain of missions along its lower reaches, where he encouraged ex-slaves from Sierra Leone to settle. These have an instructive history. The first churches in what is now Nigeria were established, not by missionaries, but by Yoroba speaking recaptive ex-slaves and their children from Sierra Leone. At the very time that *Bleak House* was published (1852-3) these Africans had returned to their homelands, where they spoke the language, and had established cotton plantations and trade with Britain on the banks of the Niger! It was they who had brought with them the faith that they had learned in Sierra Leone.[12] Buxton's vision of Christianity, Commerce and Civilisation was beginning to be realised as a genuine alternative to the Slave Trade and a revolutionary new Christian culture, formed by Africans, was appearing on African soil.

Missionaries continued to come forward bravely for this dangerous work. When the first Principal of the Church Missionary Society training college at Islington announced to the students that 'The Committee have just received tidings that six more men have been removed from their posts at Sierra Leone by death, and two by dangerous attacks of fever. I am instructed to ask whether there are any of our number who will volunteer to supply the vacancies'. Four men stepped forward immediately and two more the next day.[13] The expedition had increased, rather than discouraged, missionary, and with it educational, effort in West Africa. Perhaps happily, it may have delayed foreign commercial exploitation of the region by emphasising the health hazards, but wholesome trade by Africans with Europe was given a big boost by the expedition.

David Livingstone and Imperialism

It is also notable that David Livingstone, while a medical student, had been present at the Exeter Hall meeting in 1840 and that he, for the rest of his life, emphasised 'Christianity, Commerce and Civilisation' as the keys to helping Africa and defeating the Slave Trade in East Africa. In this he echoed Buxton, even if we do not know if he owed that vision to Buxton and the Exeter Hall meeting in the first place. The fact is that before long such emphases were almost taken for granted. Even *The Times* was soon to be printing Livingstone's journals with unqualified enthusiasm. Livingstone concluded his rather famous address to the Senate House at Cambridge with the words: 'I go back to Africa to try to make an open path for commerce and Christianity; do you carry out the work which I have begun. I leave it with you'. As Professor Walls put it: 'there is a straight line from Buxton to Livingstone'.[14] Livingstone also fully shared Buxton's confidence in the ability of Africans, which brought him into conflict with the 'Boers', who usually opposed him for this reason and on one occasion stole all his household goods and burnt his house. When stripped of their missionary aspect and secularised these aims come very near to modern ideas of 'development'. Livingstone's extraordinary journeys were chiefly to find routes for trade that would defeat the East African Slave Trade. He saw the rivers as the main ways of communication, commerce and evangelisation and therefore tried to map out their routes to the seas. His chief opponents in East Africa were the slavers, both white and black, as it must be remembered that African chiefs were deeply involved in the Trade as long as there was a good market.

There has been much written about the relationship between missions and imperialism and this is not the place to pursue it, but in a recent book the historian, Brian Stanley, explores the issue.[15] Temperley also comments on it more briefly in his study of the Niger Expedition.[16] Stanley shows that the Missionary Societies usually tried to keep themselves quite distinct from commerce and from any attempts by governments at conquest. The Secretary of the CMS, Henry Venn (a son of John Venn, the Vicar of Clapham), for instance, sought the help of cotton and other merchants for the development of trade with West Africa, but he was careful to do this in a private capacity, and even without the knowledge of most of his committee, lest the Society be regarded as having a commercial function. As early as 1859 Venn reports that: 'There are now between 200 and 300 (cotton) gins at work in Abeokuta....chiefly in the hands of Natives. Cotton is flowing to England in a stream that is widening every day.'[17]

Buxton and his allies had a policy that is easily misunderstood today and easily distorted when robbed of its primary Christian emphasis. Aspects of it, when isolated, lent themselves to crude commercial gain and imperialism. They were however inspired by genuine concern to help Africa and Africans. In the long run what they achieved in the abolition of the Trade and then the liberation of the slaves was dramatically for the good of Africa and its people, as they had hoped and expected. It has been argued that liberation was in some ways more important than the end of the British Trade. But it could not have been accomplished if Clarkson and Wilberforce and their allies had not started the whole process of attack on this ghastly evil. Neither group could foresee some of the problems, or realised how difficult the task was to which they had made a first contribution. It was far from all over when they died, but these two political victories were of huge historical significance. The victories in these two campaigns have been described as 'defining moments' in the history of the century.

Buxton, Henry Venn and Livingstone represent a concern for commerce, firstly because it was a rival to the Slave Trade, which was destroying Africa and preventing any sort of progress, evangelism or even stable social life. Much of the African leadership was preoccupied with the Trade and feeding its demands through tribal warfare to capture slaves. Secondly, contrary to most contemporary opinion, they believed in the equal ability of Africans if given the opportunity. When Livingstone was sent money by Baroness Burdett-Coutts, he replied that he hoped to use it to set up a training institution in technical skills for promising young Africans, just as Buxton would have wished.

Thirdly they really believed that wholesome trade and education would improve the lot of the people and enable them to create a more prosperous, peaceful and stable community. That in itself was a worthy Christian aim, as Africa was seen as extremely backward and unstable. If the abolition of the Trade could save Africa from becoming one vast slave farm for Europe, the development of wholesome trade could raise the standards of life to something much more satisfactory for people who were, in the eyes of Christians at least, of equal value to God and of equal capacity for development. Sierra Leone, 'the province of freedom', exemplified this and, when its educated representatives appeared in Britain, the vision seemed possible of rapid fulfilment.

Missions were, however, constantly faced with the fact that commerce was quickly divorced from any Christian concern and turned into exploitation and before long imperialism intruded into the picture. Buxton can never be charged with imperialism, indeed that concept was hardly alive in his lifetime, though it became powerful later. Imperialism developed in the second half of the Nineteenth Century and was greatly stimulated by the Indian Mutiny of 1857, which was portrayed in public as showing that subject peoples were morally inferior and needed to be ruled into civilised ways – even by a morally very dubious British Army.

It is a modern problem as to how far aid to developing countries should be tied to trade, because if it is not then governments have greater difficulty in justifying aid in many circles. Moral concern alone is not always sufficient to bring in the cash, or indeed to ensure that it is well spent. Interwoven with Buxton's other motives for stressing the value of commerce was the desire to gain support from those who were not moved by philanthropy. He felt that he had to answer economic arguments with economic arguments. This was a factor in the publicity for the Niger expedition, but his great vision was for Africa to raise itself by its own efforts and using its own resources. In 1842 he was repeating his conviction that: 'if the task of civilising and converting Africa were ever to be accomplished it would be by the agency of Africans themselves'. Therefore he was proposing a theological seminary in Sierra Leone.[18]

It can be argued in retrospect that Buxton and his allies would have done better to launch a much smaller expedition, without the massive publicity and involvement of dignitaries of the state, to see what could be achieved first on a small scale. To gain the support of the great an emphasis on the commercial opportunities was given in a way that backfired when the expedition failed. On the other hand it was this high profile of the expedition that helped to put the idea of Buxton's triple programme – Christianity, Commerce and Civilisation – into an accepted part of the thinking of many Christian leaders. The wide acceptance of such a view was represented by Livingstone and his priorities have been called 'pure Buxtonism'.[19] Buxton did not invent it, though he gave it fresh life by stressing it as the only remaining remedy for the Slave Trade.

In this connection it is interesting to record that the first West African Doctor trained in Western medicine, James Africanus Beale Horton, (see p61) went on to gain his F.R.C.S. and M.D. in London. Then after joining the British Navy he rose to be the Chief Medical Officer for the West African squadron with a rank equivalent to Colonel. When he retired to Sierra Leone, with a generous pension, he used his money both to set up a training College for African Pastors and also to found the Commercial Bank of West Africa.[20] That was exactly as Buxton would have wished, combining Christianity and commerce as twin remedies for the situation, and it was an African's initiative. It can be argued that as missionary work developed there was a tendency to delay giving Africans the same sort of leadership that had been made necessary by malaria in these early stages – that is until political independence again made it necessary. If Buxton had lived longer he might have been able to influence the Missionary Societies into trusting indigenous leadership more. His public reputation and his influence, sadly never recovered from the failure of the expedition. That would not have mattered greatly to him, but today some are rediscovering his importance and wish that some of his emphases had taken deeper root at the time.

To Buxton and his allies it was all straightforward. They had a vision of a free African people in Africa itself and in the Colonies, enjoying the benefits of Christian education, Christian faith, fair and profitable commerce in local resources and all the advantages of the good things that Europe was enjoying. That European prosperity they believed was in considerable measure due to the Christian traditions that had moulded society. Surely it was a duty to give others the benefit of these good things if possible. This, as he put it, should be done by 'calling out the resources of Africa' and he believed that it could surely be achieved and must be worked for tirelessly.

Although Britain has some horrible skeletons in its cupboard of Colonial history records, these two relatively unselfish campaigns over slavery have had an influence for good still into the twentieth century. They have strengthened the conviction that moral issues can be made to overrule economic issues and political expediency. They have given a greater sense of national conscience about how subject communities or developing countries should be dealt with, and there is no disputing the enormous benefits that came from the abolition of the Slave Trade and the Liberation Act to a huge population and at enormous cost to the Treasury. Also let it be repeated that the results were achieved peacefully and not by bloody revolution or civil war. Buxton would have wanted future generations to take courage about what can be achieved on moral grounds, even in the face of great vested interests and political obstruction, but only if there is the motivation and the will to persevere.

Notes

Chapter 1 – Wilberforce, Clarkson, Buxton and Liberation
1. Anthony Benezet published several books on the subject. This one was entitled: *Historical Account of Guinea....with an enquiry into the Rise and Progress of the Slave Trade.*
2. See Ellen Gibson Wilson. *Thomas Clarkson: A Biography*. William Sessions, York, 1989. For a more popular volume: Zebranoo Gifford. *Thomas Clarkson and the Campaign against Slavery*. Anti-Slavery International, 1996.
3. See John Pollock. *Wilberforce*. Constable, 1997, though references in the literature are frequently to Sir Reginald Coupland's *Wilberforce*. Collins, 1923 and 1945.
4. Quoted by John Pollock *op cit.*, p.283.
5. June 26th, 1924. Copied in Buxton papers held by the Rhodes House Library in Oxford.
6. G.M. Trevelyan. *English Social History*. Longmans Green, 1942, pp496-7.
7. See biographies of Shaftesbury such as G. Battiscombe. *Shaftesbury: A Biography of the Seventh Earl*. London, 1974 or John Pollock. *Shaftesbury: The Poor Man's Earl*. London, 1985.
8. Quoted by E.M. Howse. *Saints in Politics ; 'The Clapham Sect' and the Growth of Freedom*. Open University and Allen and Unwin, 1953, p184.
9. See D.Hempton. 'Evangelicalism and Reform' in *Evangelical Faith and Public Zeal: Evangelicals and Society in Britain 1780-1980*. Ed. John Wolffe, SPCK, 1995.

Chapter 2 – Home, University and Quaker Influences
1. Charles Buxton. *Memoirs of Sir Thomas Fowell Buxton, Bart.* Third edition John Murray, 1849. There are many editions of this book, but the third is an expanded edition and largely identical with the American edition of the same date (Henry Longstreth, Philadelphia). As most editions have the date in

the running title at the top of each page, making it easy to locate a quotation, page references will not be given in future unless they are out of date order. This also avoids many interruptions of the text by footnotes. All unattributed quotations will refer to this book, which is a mine of detailed information and selections from letters and memoranda. Charles had access to the very well arranged papers now at Rhodes House, Oxford and his Memoirs contains a very large number of quotations from them. His Memoirs was also translated into German, in an abstract Published 1854 (A.v.Triskow. Berlin) and a fuller version in 1855 (B.Brandis. Hamburg).

2. *ibid*, p17.
3. The practice of dis-fellowshipping or disowning was discontinued before long and it seems that she somehow avoided the formality.
4. See James Walvin. *The Quakers: Money and Morals*. John Murray, 1977
5. C. Buxton, *op cit.*, p.15
6. Augustus Hare. *The Gurneys of Earlham*. 2 Vols. Vol.1. p271, George Allen, London, 1895. This gives very full picture of their familly life, with numerous quotations from letters.
7. A. Hare, *op cit.*, Vol. 1, p46.
8. He was the nephew of George the Third and became Duke of Gloucester in 1807 and an important help in anti-slavery matters.
9. J.B. Braithwaite. *Memoirs of Joseph John Gurney*. Headley Brothers, London, 1902.
10. Janet Witney. *Elizabeth Fry: Quaker Heroine*. Harrap, 1937, p.233.
11. His Olney Hymns, including the still well known 'Amazing Grace' were written when he was vicar of Olney. He was at this time Vicar of the City church of St Mary Woolnoth. See: *Memorials of Hannah Lady Buxton*: from papers collected by her Granddaughters. Bicker and Son, London, 1833.
12. A. Hare, *op cit.*, Vol. I, pp.88-89.
13. J.B. Braithwaite, *op cit*. He had considerable influence amongst Quakers in America, one group of them being known as Gurneyites. He became a major Quaker theologian, contending when necessary for an orthodox Christian position and leading the decision to expel one who held Unitarian views. Most Quakers could at that time be called evangelical, though

their theological position was different from that of the evangelicals in the Church of England to whom the term was chiefly applied then.
14. From a manuscript letter in private hands now to be deposited in the Buxton archive at Rhodes House.
15. The University, in Common with Oxford and Cambridge, had the right to elect its own Member of Parliament.

Chapter 3 – Marriage, Employment and Christian Faith
1. William Allen, a well to do Quaker in East London, was one of the founders of the originally Quaker Pharmaceutical firm of Allen and Hanbury, which is now part of Glaxo. He was a lecturer at University College, London and a Fellow of the Royal Society. He had numerous philanthropic interests and was important in anti-slavery matters all his life. Universal primary education was not available until the Education Act of 1870, which was carried through Parliament by the Liberal MP, W.E. Forster, who was, significantly, Buxton's nephew.
2. The Bible Society was founded in 1804 on a non-denominational basis.
3. C. Buxton, *op cit.*, under the year 1810, see Ref.1 to Chapter 2 for explanation of omission of page references.
4. The Church Missionary Society (CMS) was founded in 1799, and had virtually no support from the Church of England's official leaders, many of whom opposed it. Its main support at that stage came from parish clergy and laymen. Pratt was its first Secretary. Charles Simeon was influential in its creation and it soon became the largest Anglican Missionary Society. CMS also became a lifelong interest for Buxton, who later spoke a number of times at its Annual Meetings etc.
5. *Memorials of Hannah Lady Buxton, op cit.*
6. *Memorials of Hannah Lady Buxton, op cit.*, p.33.
7. R.H. Mottram. *Buxton the Liberator.* Hutchinson, no date but evidently 1946. Mottram singularly fails to understand Buxton's ability to hold together his rather introspective piety and his practical activism. He is also critical of Buxton's orthodox theology and so fails to understnd some of his motivation.
8. In the virtual absence of public health provisions the Hospitals were largely dependent on charity. The London Hospital served the poor in the East End of London and several rela-

tives were substantial supporters, as he probably was also. It was not far from his brewery.
9. A. Hare, *op cit.*, vol.1, p.318.
10. J. Whitney. *Elizabeth Fry: Quaker Heroine.* G. Harrap, 1937.
11. J. Whitney, *op cit.*, p.235.

Chapter 4 – In Parliament
1. Dr Stephen Lushington was a very able lawyer and had been a Fellow of All Souls, Oxford. He had only entered Parliament in 1806, but he spoke on one of the key Slave Trade debates and continued as an MP to 1841. He became a close collaborator with Buxton, a real friend and his most important colleague in Parliament, though he did not take such a high profile in public.
2. See H. Potter, *Hanging in Judgment: Religion and the Death Penalty in England.* SCM Press, 1993.
3. Sir James Mackintosh, unlike most of the Liberation Party, was a 'free thinker' in religion, but an enthusiastic supporter of this and a number of other moral causes.
4. *The Banville Diaries: Journals of a Norfolk Gamekeeper 1822-44.* Ed. Norma Virgoe and Susan Yaxley. Collins, 1986.
5. This translates 'The gods in response to the prayers of the owners, obligingly wreck entire households'. He was quoting from Juvenal. *The Satires.* Satire 10, lines 8-9 in OUP World's Classics series, 1992.
6. Asa Briggs. *The Age of Improvement 1783-1867.* Longmans, 1959. Folio Society edition p.196.
7. See for instance Standish Meacham. *Henry Thornton of Clapham 1760-1815.* Harvard University Press, 1964; M.M. Hennell. *John Venn and the Clapham Sect.* Lutterworth Press, 1958; E.M. Howse. *Saints in Politics: The 'Clapham Sect' and the Growth of Freedom.* Open University and George Allen and Unwin, 1952 and biographies of Wilberforce and other members of the group.

Chapter 5 – The Liberation Cause Adopted
1. Suffield was one of the leading Whigs in the House of Lords, which was very much dominated by Tories.
2. Dictionary of National Biography. Denman (1779-1854) was an MP from 1819-1826 and 1830-32, when he became Lord Chief Justice.

3. Dictionary of National Biograhy. Brougham (1779-1868), was a Scottish MP from 1810 until he was made Lord Chancellor in 1830. He became an embittered man and was somewhat feared in Parliament for his devastating speeches.
4. See M.M. Hennel. *John Venn and the Clapham Sect*. Lutterworth, 1958.
5. E.M. Howse has an Appendix in his book *Saints in Politics, op. cit.*, on the origin of the name Clapham Sect and its history. It was made popular, and probably coined, by Sir James Stephen in an essay in 1844 after those concerned had nearly all died.
6. See: Standish Meacham. *Henry Thornton of Clapham 1760-1815, op cit*.
7. E.M. Howse, *op cit.*, p.23.
8. I am indebted to Professor Andrew Walls for permission to quote his verbal comments and to quote from his as yet unpublished 1997 'Easneye Lectures' on Thomas Fowell Buxton.
9. See Andrew Walls. 'A Christian Experiment: The Early Sierra Leone Colony.' in *The Mission of the Church and the Propagation of the Faith*. Ed G.J. Cuming. CUP, 1970.
10. These were James Africanus Beale Horton and Broughton Davies. See p.141 for Beale's career.
11. See Hugh Taylor. *The Slave Trade: The History of the Atlantic Slave Trade 1440-1870*. Picador (Macmillan), 1997 for a very detailed history of the worldwide Trade. See also H. Temperley. *British Anti-Slavery 1833-1870*. Longman, 1972.
12. Sir Reginald Coupland. *Wilberforce, op cit.*, p.282.
13. Ford K Brown. *Fathers of the Victorians: The Age of Wilberforce*. Cambridge University Press, 1961.
14. H. Temperley. *British Anti-Slavery, op cit.*, has a detailed summary of the numerous and confusing Anti-Slavery organisations in an Appendix p.271-2.
15. Temperley, *op cit.*, p.276. He writes: 'The economic changes.....were important to the extent that they removed obstacles which stood in the humanitarians' way. British governments were prepared to go along with the attack on slavery so long as they could be assured that they would not have to sacrifice too much in the process. In 1807 and 1833 this was done and they bowed to the humanitarians' demands.' See also R. Anstey. *The Atlantic Slave Trade and British Abolition*. London, 1875. Similar points are made by Robin

Blackburn in *The Overthrow of Colonial Slavery 1776-1848*. Verso (New Left Books) 1988, in spite of his major stress on the economic factors in the process.

Chapter 6 – Parliamentary Battles, Chiefly on Slavery

1. The Jamaica Journal, quoted by Charles Buxton in his 'Memoirs' of his father.
2. The London Missionary Society was founded in 1795 on an interdenominational basis, but gradually came to be regarded as mainly the organ of the Congregational Churches, as the Anglicans, Methodists and Baptists each developed their own societies.
3. E. MacInnes. *Extracts from Priscilla Johnston's Journal and Letters*, C. Thurman and Sons, Carlisle, 1862, p.11. No author's name is printed and it was presumably for private circulation as it has the name only in handwriting. In Quaker parlance at that time 'interesting' meant moving or emotionally stimulating.
4. I am indebted to a degree dissertation on *Hull and the Slave Trade* by Graham Frith.
5. D. Hempton. 'Evangelicalism and Reform, 1780-1820' in *Evangelical Faith and Public Zeal*. SPCK, 1995, p.20-21.
6. The reintroduction of the Capercailye (usually spelt Capercaillie today) is often attributed to Lord Bredalbane, who had been his host. In fact it was Buxton's idea and he brought it about. He had also introduced some of them onto his land in Norfolk, but they did not survive long there, while they did very well in Perthshire on Lord Bredalbane's estate.
7. C. Silvester Horne. *David Livingstone*. Macmillan, 1912, p.24.

Chapter 7 – The Final Battle on Slavery

1. The petition was presumably because so many forgers went free under the system and were able to do it again somewhere else. Juries would not find them guilty.
2. Norma Virgoe and Susan Yaxley. *The Banville Diaries, Journals of a Norfolk Gamekeeper 1822-44*. Collins, 1986, p.126-129. Other labourers emigrated to America from Norfolk, seeing the end of their jobs in sight.

3. See the list of Anti-slavery Societies and their dates in the Appendix to H. Temperley. *British Anti-Slavery 1832-1870.* Longman, 1972.
4. George Stephen. *Anti-slavery Recollections in a series of letters to Mrs Harriet Beecher Stowe.* Hatchard, London, 1854.
5. The proceedings are described by Priscilla in her Journal: E. MacInnes. *Extracts from Priscilla Johnston's Journal and Letters.* Charles Thurman, 1862, p.75-77 and from another point of view in *The Banville Diaries, op cit.*, p.134-135.
6. Buxton Papers at Rhodes House, Vol. 39.
7. Charles Buxton. *Memoirs, op. cit.*, 1835.
8. C. Buxton. *Memoirs,* under 1836.
9. H. Temperley, 1972, *op cit.*, p.41.

Chapter 8 – A Final Attack on the Continuing Slave Trade
1. M.M. Hennel. *Sons of the Prophets, op cit.*, p.95 in the chapter on James Stephen.
2. T.F. Buxton. *The Slave Trade and its Remedy* gives detailed figures and calculations based on official reports.
3. A. Walls. 1997 Easneye Lectures and also A. Walls. 'The Legacy of Thomas Fowell Buxton' in the International Bulletin of Missionary Research' 15. (April 1991) p.74-77.
4. There were several editions of the first part before the fuller version appeared. Quotations are from the 1840 2nd. edition of the full version.
5. A Walls. Lectures, *op cit.* He describes how little was known about Africa.
6. See M.M. Hennel, *op cit.*, for some references and Note 6 to Chapter 4.
7. E. Stock. *History of the Church Missionary Society.* Published by C.M.S. Three Vols, 1899.
8. There is a letter in the Buxton papers at Rhodes House from Russell to Buxton openly acknowledging his part in the Expedition and sharing the blame for its failure. Buxton Papers. Vol 20A, p.113, June 23rd, 1842.
9. H. Temperley. *White Dreams, Black Africa: The Antislavery Expedition to the Niger 1841-1842,* Yale University Press, 1991.
10. Hugh Thomas. *The Slave Trade: The History of the Atlantic Slave Trade 1440-1870.* Picador, 1977.
11. *ibid.*

12. Quoted by H. Temperley 1991, *op cit.*, page 61.
13. Quoted *ibid*, p.164.
14. A. Walls. Easneye Lectures, *op cit.*
15. Two books by Verily Anderson. *The Northrepps Grandchildren.* Hodder, 1968 and *Friends and Relations: Three Centuries of Quaker Families*. Hodder, 1980, give a lively picture of their home life in Norfolk. As one of Buxton's descendants she had access to numerous unpublished family papers. There is also a good description of Buxton's character in George Stephen. *Anti-slavery recollections in a series of letters to Mrs Harriet Beecher Stowe*. Hatchard, 1854.
16. A Manuscript letter from Buxton to an unnamed friend; in private hands.
17. Eugene Stock. *History of the Church Missionary Society*. Vol. 1, p.336-7. C.M.S., 1899.

Chapter 9 – Long Term Results of Liberation and the Niger Expedition

1. It was, for instance, observed on some plantations how many of the children of young slaves bore a striking likeness to the plantation manager, since he could sleep with as many girls as he liked.
2. A. Walls gives details in his 1997 Easneye Lectures on *The Legacy of Thomas Fowell Buxton*. In preparation for publication. Quoted by permission.
3. James Walvin, *Black Ivory: A History of British Slavery*. Harper Collins (Fontana), 1993, p.327, states that there were only 7,000 Indian 'coolies' in the West Indies by 1841, though many more in Mauritius.
4. See the discussion in H. Temperley, *British Anti-Slavery 1833-1870*, 1972, *op cit.*
5. Published John Murray. Charles Buxton, gives detailed and carefully checked figures for the sugar trade over the years to 1856.
6. H. Temperley in his 1972 book, *op cit.*, has a chapter devoted to the Sugar Trade in these years and the problems that the subsidy created for the anti-slavery groups.
7. E.M. Howse. *Saints in Politics, op cit.*, p.184 and M.M. Hennell. *Sons of the Prophets*. SPCK, 1979, p.21.

8. H. Temperley. *White Dreams, Black Africa.* Yale University Press, 1991, p.169-170.
9. quoted by H. Temperley, *ibid*, p.61.
10. Eugene Stock. *History of the Church Missionary Society* Vol. 1, p.455.
11. Buxton Papers at Rhodes House, Vol. 4, p.413.
12. A. Walls. Easneye Lectures 1997, *op cit.*
13. Eugene Stock. *History of the Church Missionary Society.* C.M.S., Vol. 2, p.75.
14. A. Walls. Lectures, *op cit.*
15. B. Stanley. *The Bible and the Flag.* Apollos, 1990.
16. H. Temperley. *White Dreams, Black Africa.* Yale University Press, 1991, Epilogue p.165-178.
17. Eugene Stock, *op cit.*, Vol. 2, p.110-111.
18. Buxton papers at Rhodes House. Vol. 20A, p.66.
19. A. Walls. Lectures, *op cit.*
20. *ibid.*

Bibliography

NINETEENTH CENTURY SOURCES

Buxton, Charles. Ed. *Memoirs of Sir Thomas Fowell Buxton. Bart. with a selection of his correspondence.* Second enlarged edition 1849. Murray, London and a separate edition Longstreth, Philadelphia, USA also 1849. Also 'New Edition'. Murray 1882, with an essay on 'Results of Emancipation'.

Buxton, Hannah. *Memorials of Hannah Lady Buxton from Papers Collected by her Granddaughters.* Printed for Private Circulation. Bickers, London 1883.

Buxton, Thomas Fowell. Collected papers. 45 folders in Scrap Book style with a separately bound detailed index. Deposited at the Rhodes House Library, Oxford in 1975 with a few additional letters added by members of his family in 1999.

Buxton, Thomas Fowell. *The African Slave Trade and its Remedy.* Murray, London 1840.

Hare, Augustus. *The Gurneys of Earlham.* Two Vols. George Allen 1895.

Johnston, Priscilla. *Extracts from Priscilla Johnston's Journal and Letters.* Thurman, Carlisle 1862. No author but this copy inscribed by hand and signed personally as 'Collected by her daughter E. MacInnes'. Priscilla Johnston was T.F. Buxton's daughter. Produced presumably for private circulation.

Stephen, George. *Anti-slavery Recollections in a series of letters to Mrs Harriet Beecher Stowe.* Hatchard, London 1854.

Stock, Eugene. *History of the Church Missionary Society.* 3 Vols. C.M.S. London 1899.

TWENTIETH CENTURY SOURCES

Anderson, Verily. *The Northrepps Grandchildren.* Hodder and Stoughton 1968.

Anderson, Verily. *Friends and Relations: Three Generations of Quaker Families.* Hodder and Stoughton 1980.

Anstey, Roger. *The Atlantic Slave Trade and British Abolition.* London 1975.

Braithwaite, J.B. *Memoirs of Joseph John Gurney.* London and New York 1902.

Blackburn, Robin. *The Overthrow of Colonial Slavery 1776-1841.* Verso (New Left Books) 1988.

Brown, Ford K. *Fathers of the Victorians.* Cambridge University Press 1961.

Carr-Gomm, F.C. *Handbook of the Administrations of Great Britain During the Nineteenth Century.* 2nd. Edition, Smith, Elder and Co. London 1901.

Coupland, Sir Reginald. *Wilberforce.* Collins 1945.

Gifford, Zerbanoo. *Thomas Clarkson and the Campaign against Slavery.* Anti-Slavery International 1996.

Hennell, M.M. *John Venn and the Clapham Sect.* Lutterworth 1958.

Hennell, M.M. *Sons of the Prophets: Evangelical Leaders of the Victorian Church.* SPCK 1979. This includes Chapters on T.F. Buxton, James Stephen Jnr and Henry Venn.

Howse, E.M. *Saints in Politics: The 'Clapham Sect' and the Growth of Freedom.* University of Toronto Press 1952, also Allen and Unwin and the Open University 1953.

Meacham, Standish. *Henry Thornton of Clapham.* Harvard University Press 1964.

Midgley, Clare. *Women Against Slavery: The British Campaign 1780-1870.* Routledge 1992.

Mottram, R.H. *Buxton the Liberator.* Hutchinson, no date but 1945 or 1946.

Pollock, John. *Wilberforce.* Constable 1977.

Pollock, John. *Shaftesbury: The Poor Man's Earl.* Hodder and Stoughton 1985.

Stanley, Brian. *The Bible and the Flag: Protestant missions and British imperialism in the nineteenth and twentieth Centuries.* Apollos 1990.

Temperley, Howard. *British Anti Slavery 1833-1876.* Longman 1972.

Temperley, Howard. *White Dreams, Black Africa: The Antislavery expedition to the Niger.* Yale University Press 1991.

Thomas, Hugh, *The Slave Trade: The History of the Atlantic Slave Trade 1440-1870.* Simon and Schuster, New York and Picador, London 1997.

Virgoe, Norma and Yaxley, Susan (Ed.) *The Banville Diaries: Journals of a Norfolk Gamekeeper 1822-44.* Collins 1986.

Walls, Andrew. F. *1997 Easneye Lectures.* In process of publication.

Walls, Andrew. F. *A Christian Experiment: The early Sierra Leone Colony*, in 'The Mission of the Church and the Propagation of the Gospel'. Cambridge University Press 1970.

Walvin, James. *Black Ivory: A History of British Slavery.* London 1993.

Walvin, James. *The Quakers: Money and Morals.* John Murray 1997.

Whitney, Janet. *Elizabeth Fry: Quaker Heroine.* Harrap 1937.

Wilson, Ellen Gibson. *Thomas Clarkson: A Biography.* William Sessions, York 1988.

Wolffe, John. (Ed.) *Evangelical Faith and Public Zeal: Evangelicals and Society in Britain 1780-1980.* SPCK 1995.

Index

AFRICAN Institution 48, 63
Agency Committee 85-87, 96, 103, 119, 120 *and see* Sturge
Albert, Prince 113, 121, 122, 137
Allen, William 9, 30, 63, 145
Althorp, Lord 87, 89, 92, 95, 97
Anglicans: 73, 96, 105
   High Church 14, 30, 105, 119, 135
   Evangelical 16, 21, 63 *and see* Simeon, Church Missionary Society and Pratt
Antigua 103, 133
Anti-slavery Committee (Quaker) 4
Anti-slavery Reporter 85
Anti-slavery societies 147;
   Anti-Slavery Society 9, 63, 86, 96 *see* Universal Abolition Society
Anti-slavery International 107
Apprenticeship 97-98, 103-105
Ashley, Lord *see* Shaftesbury
Australia 44, 83, 84

BABINGTON, Thomas 43, 56-57, 59
Bahamas 107
Baptists 4, 60, 63
Barbados 69, 73
Benezet, Anthony 4-5, 143

Bermuda 103, 133
Bible Society 30, 40, 41, 55, 100, 105
Birmingham 85, 107
Bishops 10, 125, of London 41, 115, 119
Brazil 61, 65, 86, 119, 125
Brewery (Brick Lane) 28-30, 36, 48, 88
Bristol 3, 89
Brougham, Henry 48, 55, 70-72, 91, 105
Buxton, Charles viii, 134, 143-144
Buxton, Hannah (nee Gurney) 24-26, 29, 31-34
Buxton, Priscilla 55, 79, 91, 101, 128 (as Mrs Andrew Johnston) 109, 152
Buxton, Sarah Maria *see* 'Cottage Ladies'
Buxton, Thomas Fowell:
   Home and School 18-21, 30
   Friendship with Gurneys 21-25
   Quaker influences 20-27
   University 25-27
   Marriage 28
   Employment 28
   Leaves Quakers 30
   Religious Experience 31-32
   Family life 47

155

Poverty concerns 28-30,
  35-37
Education concerns 30, 37,
  48, 100
Public speeches 30, 37
Motives and Priorities 33-35,
  114-116, 127-130
Relationship to Wilberforce
  10, 38, 41-43
Urged to enter Parliament 41
Elected for Weymouth 42
Political stance 41, 42, 45, 47
Prisons 40, 41, 48
Penal reform 43-51, 55, 83
Convict ships 40, 44
Asked to lead on liberation
  and accepts 53-54
His 'team' 55-58
First motion on liberation 67
Compensation to planters 71,
  82, 96-98
Apprenticeship 97-98,
  103-107
Victory on liberation 99-101
Book on continuing Slave
  Trade 111-112
Niger Expedition projected
  107-113 and launched
  116-122
Defeated in election 105
Baronetcy 121
Death 125
Monuments in Westminster
  Abbey and Freetown 17,
  126-127
On Free Trade 88
On Protestant Ascendancy
  78, 106
Influence on Missionary
  policy 140-141
See also: Bible Society,
  Church Missionary Society,
  London City Mission,
  RSPCA, Livingstone,
  Mauritius, South Africa,
  Suttee, Gamekeepers,
  Weymouth

CANNING, George 67-71, 74,
  78, 81
Capercaillie 76, 127, 148
Capital Punishment *see* Penal
  Reform
Catholics 23, 106
Catholic Emancipation 77-78,
  105
Chalmers, Thomas 37
'Christian Observer' *see*
  Macaulay
Church Missionary Society 30,
  41, 55, 60, 116, 121, 128,
  137, 139, 145
Church of England *see* Anglicans
Clarkson, John 59, 113
Clarkson, Thomas 5-10, 56, 62,
  69, 101, 108
  Links with Quakers 5
  Approaches Wilberforce 6
  Sierra Leone 59
  Writings and leaflets 5, 57
  Tours the country 5, 53-59,
    65
  Links with Lake District poets
    5, 56
  Congratulated by Buxton 99
'Clapham Sect' 8, 55-56, 147
Coleridge, Samuel Taylor 6
Convict ships 40-44
'Cottage Ladies' 58, 79-80, 109,
  119
Cotton 111-112 123, 139
Cromer 47, 48, 70
Crowther, Samuel Ajayi 61, 121,
  123-5, 137
Cuba 61, 65, 86, 119, 120

DEATH penalty *see* Penal reform
Denman, Thomas 51, 55, 72, 74

Demerara (Guiana) 68, 72, 133
Dickens, Charles 136-137
Dominica 107
Dublin University = Trinity College (T.C.D.) 25-27, 78

EARLHAM 21-31, 34
East African Slave Trade 3, 111, 138
Edinburgh 85
Emmet, Robert 26, 46
Evangelicals 3, 16, 65 *and see* Anglicans

FERNANDO Po 112, 117, 123
Forster, William 54, 58
Forster, W.E. (son of William) 145
Fourah Bay College 61, 125, 141
Fox, Charles James 11
Free Churches 16, 58, 63, 69, 74, 78, 96, 105
French Revolution 8, 11, 14, 46, 63, 87
Fry, Elizabeth 23-30, 38-40, 45, 48

GAMEKEEPERS: in Essex (Abraham Plaistow) 19,114; in Norfolk (Banville) 47-48, 84, 88, 148
Gladstone W.E. 119
Glasgow 85
Glenelg, Lord 88, 101-102, 110, 118
Gold Coast (Ghana) 122
Gloucester, Prince and Duke 22, 63, 70,144
Goderich, Lord 78, 83, 97
Grant, Charles Snr. 56, 88
Grant, Charles Jnr. *see* Glenelg
Grey, Lord 11, 87, 88, 94

Gurney, Anna *see* 'Cottage Ladies'
Gurney, Elizabeth *see* Fry
Gurney, Hannah *see* Hannah Buxton
Gurney, John Snr. 21-23
Gurney, John Jnr. 25
Gurney, Joseph John 22-25, 30, 54, 58, 96, 144
Gurney, Priscilla 23, 48-49, 54
Gurney, Samuel 63, 119

HAITI (St. Domingue) 11, 63
Hoare, Samuel 28, 36, 37, 58, 119
Horton, James Africanus Beale 141
Hottentots *see* South Africa
Howick, Lord 92-95

IRISH Nationalists 1, 26, 74; Protestant Ascendancy 78, 106; *see* O'Connell
Irish Tithes Bill 105-106
Imperialism 130, 138-140

JAMAICA 64, 68-69, 73, 74, 89, 90, 100, 107, 133
Johnston, Andrew 79, 101, 109, 117, 133

LIBERATION Act passed 99, 101
Liberia 122
Liverpool, Lord 67-68, 78
Livingstone, David 3, 77, 135, 138-139, 141
London City Mission 41, 115
London Hospital 36, 40
London Missionary Society 69, 76, 148
Lords, House of 9, 10, 43, 52, 54, 83, 89, 90, 99, 105
Lottery 55, 62

Lushington, Stephen 43, 54-55,
    72, 73, 82, 91, 96, 97, 100,
    117, 119-120

MACAULAY, Thomas Babington
    58, 63, 92
Macaulay, Zachary 54-60, 73,
    101
    In Sierra Leone 57-60, 113
    Writings 57, 58, 85
    Buxton's assessment 57, 97
Mackintosh, Sir James 44, 51,
    72, 83
Malaria 113-114, 123, 135-136
Mansfield, Lord Chief Justice 4,
    59
Mauritius 74-76, 82, 104
Methodists 16, 58, 60-63, 69, 73
Melbourne, Lord 109-110, 117
Missionaries 60, 69, 73, 89, 137
Missionary Societies 60, 121,
    123, 132, 137-139, 140, 141,
    see also Church Missionary
    Society and London
    Missionary Society
Murray, Sir George 78, 81

NEWGATE Prison 34, 38-40
Newton, John 7, 23, 144
Niger Expedition 112-125,
    135-142
Niger River 137
Non-Conformists see Free
    Churches
Northrepps Cottage see 'Cottage
    Ladies'
Northrepps Hall 25, 47, 79-80,
    84, 99, 101, 124, 125
Nova Scotia 59

O'CONNELL, Daniel 74, 78, 83
Overstrand church and school
    80, 124,125

PALMERSTON, Lord 110, 117

Peel, Sir Robert 51, 90, 121
Penal Reform 39, 40-41, 44-51,
    83
'Peterloo Massacre' 46-47
Phillips, James 5
Pitt, William (the younger) 6-8
Portugal 61,119
Pratt, Josiah 30-31,145

QUAKERS 3-6, 20-27, 40, 43,
    59, 62, 66, 76, 86, 119
    American Quakers 4, 38
    Original Quaker Anti-Slavery
    Committee 4
    See Earlham, Phillips, Sturge,
    Wedgwood
Queen Caroline 72

REFORM Bills 78, 87-89
Results of Liberation 131-135
Results of Niger Expedition
    135-141
Russell, Lord John 117, 136, see
    note 8 on p149
RSPCA 127

ST LUCIA 72
Shaftesbury, Lord 13, 119, 131
Sharp, Granville 4-5, 59
Shoreditch see Brewery
Sierra Leone 55, 57, 59-61, 111,
    113, 122, 125, 126, 137-140
Simeon, Charles 21, 22, 36, 46,
    62, 76
South Africa 13, 48, 76-7,
    101-102, 127, 130
Spain 61, 119
Spitalfields 30, 37-38, 40, 45, 48
Stanley, Lord 97, 99, 110
Stephen, George 58, 85, 93
Stephen, James Snr. 57
Stephen, James Jnr. 58, 88, 110
Stowe, Mrs Harriet Beecher 93
Sturge, Joseph 103-107,
    119-120

INDEX

Suffield, Lord 54, 84, 87, 96-99, 104, 146
Sugar 125, 131-134, *see* note 6 on p150
Suttee 45, 54-55, 76

TEMPERLEY, Howard 64-65, 107, 118,135, 154
Thornton, Henry 8, 56, 59, 62
The Times 9, 101, 120, 126, 136-137
Tory Party 7, 75, 78, 87, 89
Trinidad 71,107

UNIVERSAL Abolition Society (UAS) 86, 103-104
USA 2,11, 59, 61,65, 86-87, 90, 120, 131, 133-134, *see* Quakers (American)

VENN, John 55, 147
Venn, Henry 139

WALES (Carmarthen) 97
Walls, Andrew 127, 138, 147
Wedgwood, Josiah 5-6
Wellington, Duke of *see* Tory Party
Wesley, John 4, 58
'West Indians' in Parliament 52, 64, 67, 71, 81, 84, 96, 98

Weymouth 28, 42, 75, 92
Whig Party 47, 75, 87
Wilberforce (the Ship) 121-123
Wilberforce, William 6-17, 43 , 48, 67, 87,89 *see also* T.F. Buxton and T. Clarkson
Enters Parliament 7
Conversion 7
Friendship with Pitt 7, 53
First motion on Slave Trade 8
Victory on Slave Trade 9
Helps Sierra Leone 59
Early desire for liberation 9
Reasons for inaction on liberation 9, 53, 54, 62
Illnesses 43, 46, 53
Asks Buxton to lead on Liberation 38, 41, 53
Last speech in Parliament 73
Leaves Parliament 73
Last pamphlet 66
Last public speech 85
Death 10, 99
Funeral 126
Wilmot, Sir Eardley 105
Windrush (the ship) 132
Woolman, John 4
Wordsworth, William 5, 56